DISEASES: FINDING THE CURE

Robert Mulcahy

The Oliver Press, Inc.
Minneapolis

Please address inquiries to:

The Oliver Press, Inc.
Charlotte Square
5707 West 36th Street
Minneapolis, MN 55416-2510

The publisher wishes to thank **Dr. Harley Geller,** Cedars-Sinai Medical Center, Los Angeles, California, for his careful review of this manuscript.

Library of Congress Cataloging-in-Publication Data

Mulcahy, Robert, 1971-
Diseases: finding the cure / Robert Mulcahy
p. cm.—(Innovators)
Includes bibliographical references and index.
ISBN 1-881508-28-5 (library binding)
1. Medical scientists—Biography—Juvenile literature. I. Title. II. Series: Innovators (Minneapolis, Minn.)
R134.M85 1996
610' .92'2—dc20
[B] 95-42739
CIP
AC

ISBN 1-881508-28-5
Innovators I
Printed in the United States of America

02 01 00 99 98 97 96 7 6 5 4 3 2 1

DISEASES: FINDING THE CURE

CONTENTS

An array of microscopes, clockwise from top left: an Italian compound microscope made before 1686; a small traveling microscope, early 1800s; a combination microscope made by John Cuthbert of London c. 1827; and a "solar" microscope from 1775. The solar model fastened over a hole in a window shutter and reflected the image onto a wall in a dark room.

INTRODUCTION

Discovering an Invisible World

The world is full of creatures so small that we cannot see them without a microscope. These microscopic creatures—called microorganisms—are everywhere: floating in the air, lying on every surface, even living inside of us. In fact, we cannot exist without them.

Not all microorganisms, however, are beneficial. There are many types of microorganisms that can make us ill. The two most dangerous are bacteria and viruses.

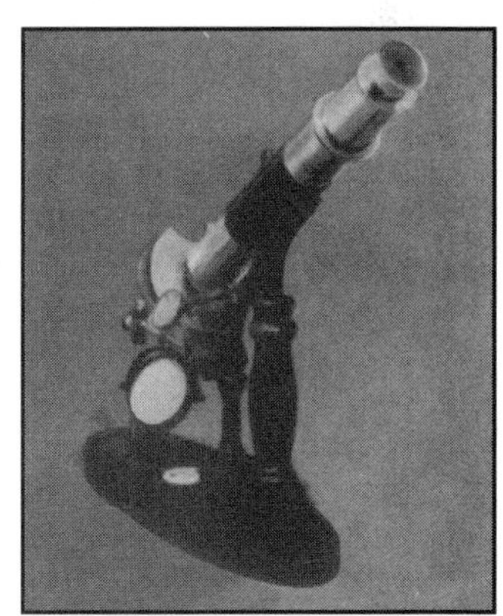

This compound microscope was devised for students in 1873.

There are thousands of kinds of bacteria. Each is only a single cell, which means bacteria are very small—only about 0.000039 inches in diameter. Some kinds of bacteria are good because they help us digest our food or kill invading microorganisms. Others, though, make us sick when they get in our bodies.

Viruses are somewhat different from bacteria. The biggest viruses, for one thing, are only one-tenth the size of the average bacterium. And unlike

bacteria: single cell creatures that can be helpful or can cause disease in plants or animals. Bacterium is the singular form of bacteria.

virus: from the Latin word for poison, this microorganism often spreads disease

some bacteria, no viruses are helpful. Instead, they can make us very ill.

For thousands of years, no one knew that tiny creatures too small to see filled the world. Without microscopes, doctors and scientists had no way of seeing viruses and bacteria. And since they could not see these tiny microorganisms, people thought that illness was supernatural. A god might punish someone with a fever. A ghost might cause an outbreak of the flu. Doctors not only gave patients medicine, they also performed rituals to drive away evil spirits.

Yet, some ancient cures helped people in very scientific ways. In Africa, certain healers treated wounds by coating them with a solution made from snake heads and ant eggs. It was not until hundreds of years later that twentieth-century scientists discovered that ant eggs contain formalin, a chemical that kills microorganisms and prevents infection.

Sometimes, however, doctors did more harm than good. Until the 1800s, many doctors bled patients because they thought that this practice allowed bad blood—or evil spirits—to leave the patient. But cutting open the skin and allowing blood to flow out of the body usually only made a sick person weaker.

Modern medicine began with a Greek physician named Hippocrates. Born on the small island of Cos in 460 B.C., Hippocrates has been called the "Father of Medicine." He was one of the first people to teach that diseases are natural and are not caused by magic or demonic spirits. Hippocrates realized that the body had amazing powers of healing and that it could cure itself of most diseases. This ancient Greek physician taught his medical students that the role of a doctor was to help the body heal itself. He believed that the worst thing a doctor could do was to interfere with the body's natural healing ability. Hippocrates's motto was "First, do no harm."

This ancient physician advised his associates to watch a patient and observe the disease's progress carefully. Hippocrates preached that the doctor must explore different possibilities until a solution, or cure, presented itself. Moreover, doctors must stand by their conclusions even when others did not believe them.

Hippocrates (460-370 B.C.), considered the father of modern medicine, was a Greek physician and teacher. The Hippocratic Oath, a code of medical ethics still used by some medical schools today, cannot be directly credited to him, but it does represent many of his ideas.

Another Greek physician, named Galen of Pergamum (130-201), became famous for incorporating the theory of the four humors—blood, yellow bile, black bile, and phlegm—into Greek medicine. Each humor originated in a specific body organ and was associated with two of four fundamental qualities—hot, dry, wet, and cold—and also with one of the four elements: air, fire, earth, and water. To cure a disease, the balance of all the humors had to be restored. For example, a disease of the blood—associated with the element of air, the heart organ, and the qualities of hot and wet—would require a dry and cold treatment, or a drug associated with those qualities, to bring the humors back into balance. In the Middle Ages (about 500 to 1500), this became the ruling medical theory and provided the rationale for such procedures as bleeding, forced vomiting, and sweating. European monks kept some

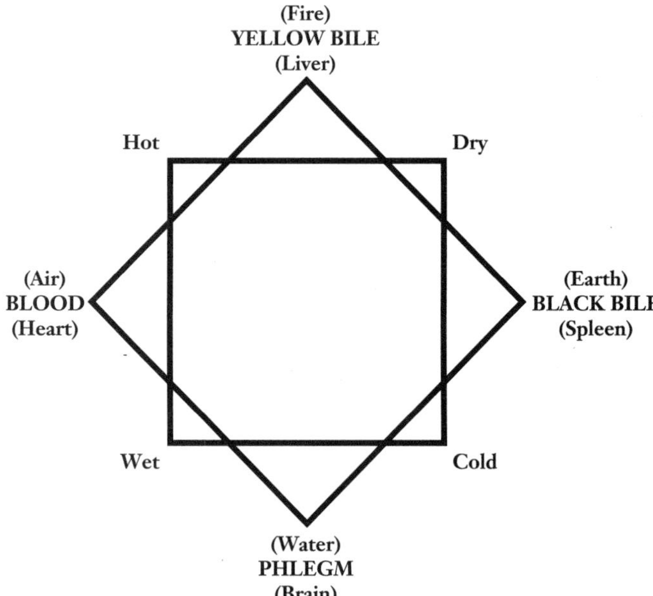

Although he was most famous for expanding on the theory of the humors, illustrated here, Galen also made many anatomical discoveries by dissecting animals.

medical knowledge alive during the Middle Ages. As a part of their religious mission, they practiced healing and helped to reconcile scientific and Christian viewpoints.

At this same time, the Arabs had translated and were using methods of ancient Greek medical texts. To this tradition, they added their new idea of medical schools and hospitals, which in the 1100s spread to Europe with the founding of medical universities such as Solarano in Italy and Montpellier in France.

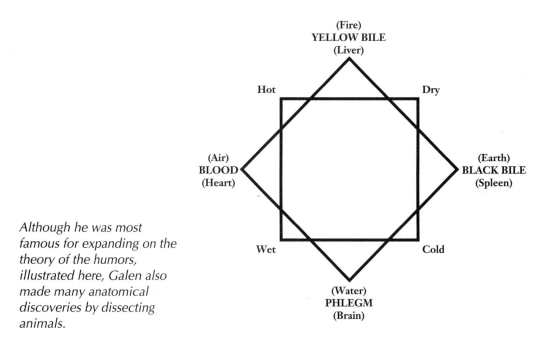

The traditional teachings of these medical schools did not, however, stop scientists from conducting their own experiments. In 1546, for example, Girolamo Fracastoro suggested that sickness was caused by tiny germs—a particular kind for each disease—that multiplied in the patient's body. But without proof, no one listened to him. At about the same time, Flemish physician Andreas Vesalius accurately mapped the human anatomy. In 1628, William Harvey published his discovery of how blood circulates through the human body. While these breakthroughs greatly increased understanding of how different organs work, thousands of doctors and scientists still followed the teachings of the ancient texts.

To aid his anatomy studies, Andreas Vesalius (1514-1564) dissected human corpses. His discoveries challenged many conventional medical teachings.

The 1600s were unique in the history of science. In 1609, Galileo Galilei gazed through a new invention called a telescope and proved what Nicolas Copernicus had theorized one hundred years before: that the earth was not the center of the universe, but revolved around the sun, as did the other planets. Physicist Isaac Newton described the three laws of motion, which explain gravity, in his 1687 book *Principia Mathematica*. Medicine, too, was ready for new scientific ideas. Shortly before his death in 1626, English philosopher Francis Bacon urged doctors and scientists to collect data and to experiment to seek new cures.

English physician William Harvey (1578-1657) demonstrated to King Charles I, one of his patients, how the heart pumps the blood.

At the beginning of the 1700s, scientists were still uncertain about the cause of disease. People knew that some diseases were contagious. But because they did not know how they spread, they could only control them through quarantine. The introduction of the microscope in the early 1600s had allowed people to see tiny parasites and bacteria, but most people believed those microorganisms were symptoms of a disease rather than the cause.

contagious or communicable disease: any disease that can be transmitted from one person or animal to another

quarantine: separating sick people from others to prevent disease from spreading

Frederick Banting signed this sketch of himself "Science has no nationality. Research is the search for truth."

Slowly, however, people began to accept new ideas and to find cures for diseases. This book is about those ideas. Naval surgeon James Lind and physician Edward Jenner showed that they could use scientific experiments to prove the truth of their theories. Their innovations not only eliminated two terrible diseases, but later allowed chemist Louis Pasteur to perform experiments that proved that living microorganisms cause disease.

In the twentieth century, scientists such as Paul Ehrlich and Jonas Salk continued to use Pasteur's theory to find treatments for two diseases that had plagued people for centuries, syphilis and polio. Alexander Fleming discovered penicillin, one of the most important medical treatments of all, growing in a petri dish. A fuzzy, blue mold, it looked like something most people would quickly discard. Instead, Fleming started experimenting with the mold. That same decade, surgeon Frederick Banting read an article about the pancreas that gave him an idea that others had missed. His insight, plus hours of work and research, resulted in the drug insulin, which has saved the lives of millions of people with diabetes. Following in the footsteps of these medical innovators, scientists today continue the work of finding the cure for the diseases that ail the human race.

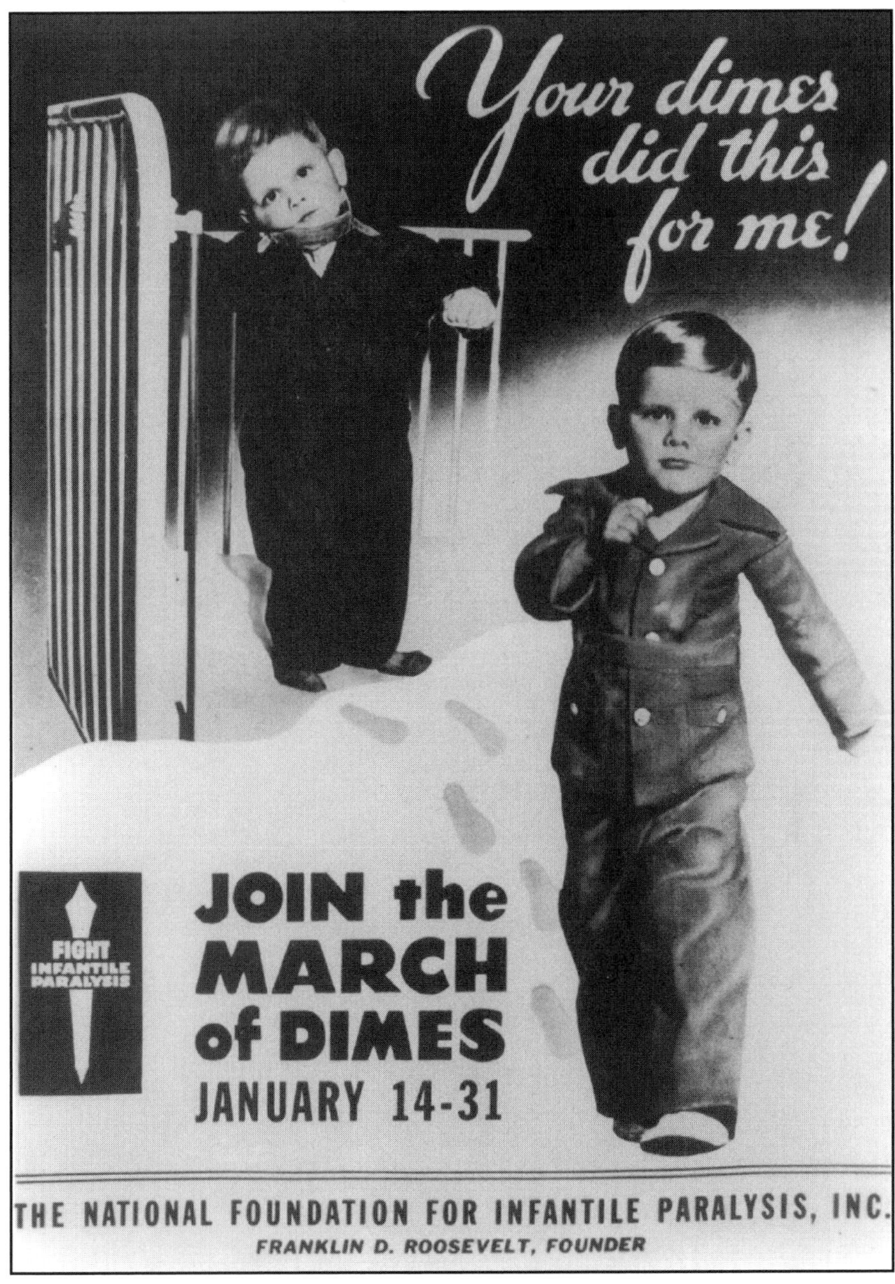

In 1938, Donald Anderson was the first March of Dimes poster child. The money raised by this organization helped fund the research for a polio vaccine.

CHAPTER ONE

James Lind and Scurvy

The high seas used to be a dangerous place. Storms, pirates, and starvation killed thousands of sailors. The biggest danger on a long sea voyage, however, was a disease called scurvy. When the Portuguese captain Vasco da Gama sailed around the Cape of Good Hope (1497-1499), half of his crew died of scurvy. The disease remained a serious threat to sailors until 1747, when naval surgeon James Lind began a famous experiment that uncovered a cure for this dreaded disease.

James Lind was born in Edinburgh, Scotland, on October 4, 1716, to Margaret and James Lind. His father earned a comfortable living as a merchant. As a boy, James became fluent in Latin, the language that scientists and scholars most often used at the time. He also knew a great deal about history, especially ancient Greece.

Dr. James Lind (1716-1794) used one of the first clinical trials ever conducted to discover a cure for scurvy.

When he was 15, Lind decided to become a doctor. His decision may have been influenced by his uncle, a successful surgeon, or perhaps he had seen the innocent victims of an epidemic of smallpox and wanted to help. Whatever the reason, Lind became an apprentice to George Langlands, a well-known Edinburgh physician.

Being an apprentice was not a glorious job, especially during the first year of his apprenticeship. Lind began his medical career by sweeping floors, washing windows, tending the fire, and carrying coal. However, he also studied all of the standard textbooks of the day, including works by the ancient Greek physician Hippocrates. As the months passed, Lind watched Langlands at work on his patients, learning the symptoms and the names of the various diseases from his observations.

After a while, the young man began to perform small medical tasks such as bandaging wounds and preparing drugs. His responsibilities grew slowly for eight years until 1739, when he was ready to practice medicine on his own. That year, Lind entered the British navy as a surgeon.

The British navy was already one of the finest in the world, and it would dominate the oceans over the next century. At that time, naval ships were made of wood with huge white flowing sails. As many as a thousand sailors crowded aboard each ship, sleeping in hammocks with only inches between them.

With no refrigeration, keeping food from spoiling was one of the biggest problems on a long voyage. Several times a week, the naval cooks served beef and pork, salted to preserve the meat. The

sailors also ate biscuits but, more often than not, weevils (small mites) infested the stale, hardened rolls. Before eating them, the sailors knocked the biscuits against their dining tables so that the weevils fell to the floor. Eventually, the biscuits became so hard that even the weevils could not eat them. While the captain and the other officers usually brought their own supply of fresh food with them, including some fruits and vegetables, the crew had to make do with only leathery meat and old biscuits.

Although stately and graceful in appearance, these wooden ships often sailed with crews that suffered from overcrowding, poor food, and a deadly disease called scurvy.

One author from the 1700s described a sailor with scurvy as follows: *"His legs swelled and pained him so that he could not walk; his flesh lost all its elasticity, so that if it was pressed in, it would not return to its shape and his gums swelled until he could not open his mouth. His breath, too, became very offensive; he lost all strength and spirit; could eat nothing; grew worse every day; and, in fact, unless something was done for him, would be a dead man in a week at the rate at which he was sinking."*

hemorrhage: profuse discharge of blood from the blood vessels; to bleed rapidly and in large amounts

The biggest threat to sailors, however, was not starvation but scurvy. Although no exact statistics are available, it is certain that during the 300 years before Lind joined the British navy, scurvy killed more sailors than wars, shipwrecks, or any other disease.

Scurvy usually struck two or three months into a voyage. After the first appearance of the symptoms of scurvy, a sailor, depending on his general health, could suffer weeks or perhaps months before he died. If the weather were cold and wet, however, the disease appeared sooner and killed more quickly.

At the time, few people recognized that the poor diet of the sailors—specifically a lack of the vitamin C found naturally in citrus fruits and vegetables such as potatoes and onions—caused scurvy. The body can store some vitamin C, but scurvy sets in after two to eight weeks without it. The disease weakens the capillaries, or small blood vessels, which causes hemorrhages into the tissues, bleeding of the gums and loosening of the teeth, anemia, exhaustion and, finally, death.

Some sailors, however, had already suspected that scurvy could be cured by eating fresh fruits and vegetables. In 1605, James Lancaster was the captain of the *Dragon*, one of four ships headed from England to the East Indies. Whenever one of his crew showed signs of scurvy, he would feed him three teaspoons of lemon juice every morning. While nearly half of the sailors on the other three ships died of scurvy, none of the 202 sailors on board the *Dragon* died.

These lemons contain an important element, ascorbic acid or vitamin C, which humans need to keep healthy. Not only does vitamin C prevent and cure scurvy, but some scientists believe it also helps prevent or alleviate symptoms of the common cold.

Unfortunately, James Lancaster was one of hundreds of people who claimed they had the cure for scurvy. Some sailors believed that drinking sea water would cure it, and others thought that cinnamon or vinegar offered the best cure. With so many supposed "cures" available, naval officers did not know what to believe.

James Lind had read and studied the history of scurvy, so he knew about many of these so-called cures. He decided that the only way to find out which of them worked was to try an experiment of his own.

THE BREAKTHROUGH

On May 20, 1747, while serving aboard the *Salisbury*, Lind began his experiment to find out which cures worked for scurvy and which did not. He selected 12 sailors who had scurvy. Each had rotting gums and spots on his skin and was weakening rapidly.

While under Lind's care, every sailor received the same basic diet. He divided the group into six pairs, and each pair of sailors was fed a different supplement with each meal. The six supplements were the most popular ways to treat scurvy at the time.

Each day, 2 of the 12 sailors had to drink a quart of apple cider, and 2 others drank 25 drops of elixir vitriol (a blend of sugar, alcohol, water, and sulfur). They were given this treatment three times a day and also had to gargle with the elixir.

Two other sailors drank two spoonfuls of vinegar three times a day and gargled with the vinegar as well. Every day, two other sailors drank half a pint of saltwater.

Three times a day, another pair of sailors ate nutmeg mixed with garlic, horseradish, and other spices. Finally, two other sailors ate one lemon and two oranges every day.

Lind took careful notes and tracked the progress of each patient. The results of his experiment quickly became obvious. In less than a week, one of the sailors who had eaten the oranges and lemons was fit for duty, and the other was on his way to recovery. The health of the two men who had drunk the cider was somewhat improved, but

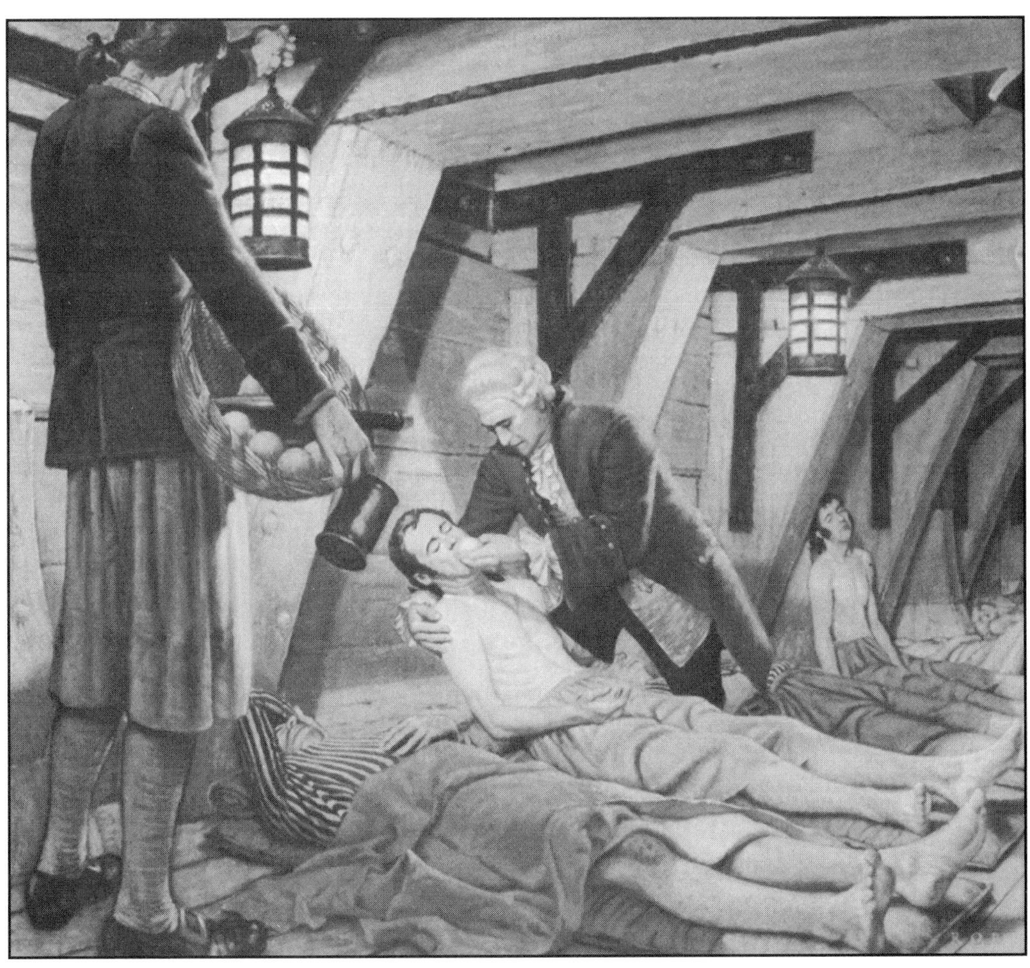

Dr. James Lind cured his patients of scurvy with fresh fruits and vegetables containing a substance not discovered until the 1900s—vitamin C.

they were still weakening. The other cures had been useless. Each of the remaining sailors was no better off than before the treatment.

Lind had proven that citrus fruits cure scurvy. He did not know, of course, that it was the vitamin C in the fruit that was the key ingredient, because vitamin C itself would not be discovered until years later. Lind did, however, continue his experiments with other fruits and vegetables and, by 1753, he had gathered enough information to write *A Treatise on the Scurvy.*

In this book, Lind recommended that sailing ships on long journeys carry a large supply of onions and sauerkraut because they last for a long period of time and would prevent scurvy. He also suggested ways of keeping fruits and fruit juice fresh on a long journey and urged that sailors' rooms be kept as dry and warm as possible, as this would also help to keep them healthy.

Lind's experiment was one of the first clinical trials. In a clinical trial, scientists give a treatment, such as a new drug, to a group of people—known as a control group—to see if it will be effective. The scientists carefully record the results of the experiment and compare these results to those of other groups. Lind's clinical trial included only 12 subjects. Today, pharmaceutical companies test new drugs with clinical trials that can include hundreds of thousands of people.

THE RESULTS

Despite Lind's findings, the British navy took almost 50 years to begin using citrus fruits for treating scurvy. A number of factors delayed the introduction of his methods. First of all, many officers did not believe in Lind's treatment, or they thought that other cures were better. Also, citrus fruits were expensive. In 1795, however, Sir Gilbert Blane, physician to the British fleet, recommended that lemon juice be served daily aboard all naval ships. Because lemon and other citrus juices were all commonly called lime juice, "limey" became a nickname for a British sailor.

The results of Blane's policy were spectacular. Before 1795, thousands of British sailors died of scurvy each year. But by 1800, only five years later, scurvy had become a rare disease. It was in part because of this ability to control scurvy that the British navy later succeeded in blockading France during the Napoleonic wars in the early 1800s.

Unfortunately, scurvy struck the British navy once again in 1875. By that time, the navy had switched to lime juice, which was cheaper than lemon juice. But lime juice contained only about one-fourth the amount of vitamin C that was found in lemons or oranges and, that year, scurvy struck the sailors of two British ships exploring in the Arctic. Outbreaks of scurvy occurred on several other vessels as well. Not until 1919 did historian Alice Henderson Smith discover that these sailors had been drinking lime juice instead of lemon juice.

Although many people thought of scurvy as a sea disease, it also appeared on land. Many people came down with the disease when the potato crops failed in Ireland and Scotland in 1846 and 1847. Soldiers during the American Civil War (1861-1865) suffered from scurvy as did the Indian, Turkish, and Australian soldiers who fought in the 1915 Gallipoli campaign during World War I. Today, however, we seldom hear of a case of scurvy.

The nutritious potato, which contains vitamin C, was an important food source for most people in Ireland when the potato blight destroyed all crops from 1845 to 1850. During that time, one and one-half million people left Ireland, mostly emigrating to Britain or North America. Another one million or more people died of starvation or diseases such as typhus, dysentery, and scurvy.

Unfortunately, James Lind did not live to see the results of his experiment. After resigning from the British navy in 1748, he returned to Edinburgh to work as a physician. He soon became the chief physician at the Royal Naval Hospital at Haslar, one of three new naval hospitals built at that time. The hospital was located near the entrance of Portsmouth harbor so that sick and injured sailors could be transported directly from their ships. Lind retired in 1783 and was succeeded by his son John.

In addition to his work on scurvy, Lind made other important innovations. One of his discoveries was the use of distillation to change sea water into fresh water. The steam from boiling sea water was perfectly fresh and needed only to be captured and cooled. Before Lind's method, a crew could be surrounded by miles of ocean water but still have nothing to drink if their ship ran out of fresh water.

Lind was also the first person to recognize that new naval recruits might carry diseases. He recommended that doctors examine all sailors before they began serving on a ship, a practice which stopped the spread of many diseases aboard ship.

Referred to as the "Father of Naval Medicine," James Lind died on July 18, 1794. As a scientist, he worked to separate fact from fiction and was not satisfied until he found the answers for himself. His experiments saved the lives of thousands of sailors.

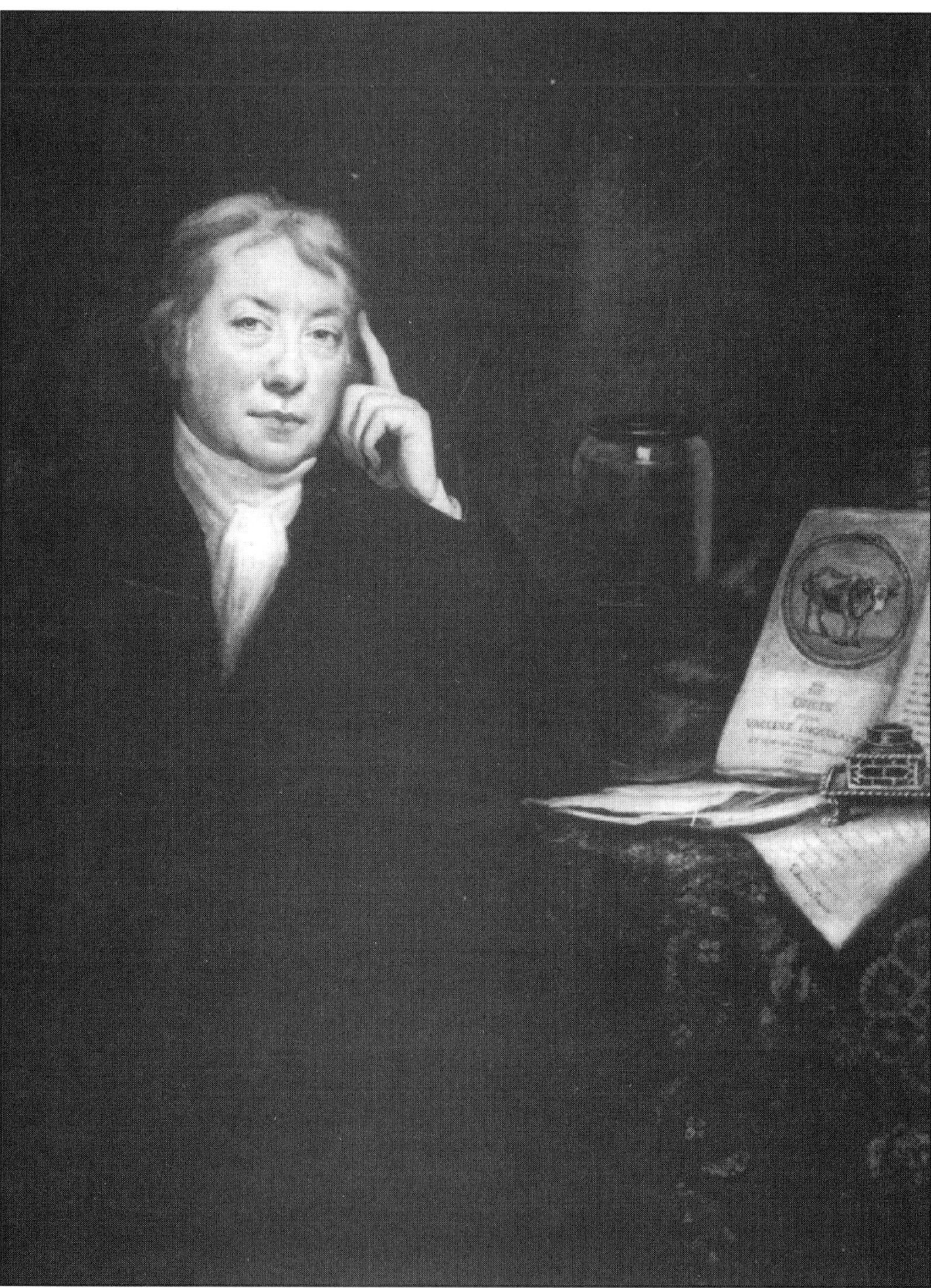

CHAPTER TWO

Edward Jenner and the Smallpox Vaccine

Smallpox is a disease that terrified people for thousands of years. During the 1700s, this disease took approximately 400,000 lives each year in Europe alone and left hundreds of thousands more living with scarred and disfigured faces. The smallpox virus could spread through a town like wildfire, bringing high fever and a blistering rash to everyone who caught it. Half of those who contracted the disease would die within weeks—and there was no cure. During the 1790s, however, a British doctor named Edward Jenner developed a technique for preventing the spread of this deadly disease.

Smallpox, which looks like a severe case of chicken pox, got its name because of the pus-filled pimples, or pustules, that develop on the faces and bodies of its victims. No one knows exactly when the first case of smallpox was contracted, but the virus was described in ancient texts from India and China as early as the twelfth century B.C.

While an apprentice doctor, Edward Jenner (1749-1823) met a farm worker who sparked Jenner's interest in discovering an inoculation against smallpox.

inoculation: the process of intentionally injecting a substance into the body to produce or increase resistance to a disease associated with that substance

The practice of inoculation was popularized in Great Britain by Lady Mary Wortley Montagu, an author who had learned about the technique while living in Turkey. Her husband served as an ambassador there from 1716 to 1718.

A 3000-year-old technique called inoculation could prevent smallpox, but it had mixed results. Doctors in ancient Asia discovered that someone who caught smallpox and survived could never catch it again. Inoculation took advantage of this phenomenon. By taking some pus from the pustule of an infected person and scratching it into a healthy person's arm, physicians could intentionally give someone a mild case of smallpox. After recovering, the patient would be immune to the disease.

Inoculation was not a perfect solution, however. Sometimes a mild case of smallpox would turn into a serious case, and the person who had been inoculated would die. Likewise, some inoculated people would accidentally spread the disease to others, and an epidemic would break out.

An individual could catch smallpox by coming in contact with someone who was infected or with the tiny flakes of skin left on that person's belongings. To guard against the disease, "inoculation stables" or "smallpox houses" were built in Britain. The people being inoculated were confined to large sheds about two miles from the nearest town for as long as two weeks, or the time it took to recover from a mild case of smallpox.

In 1757, one of the children living in a smallpox house was eight-year-old Edward Jenner. At first, Edward loved to explore the nearby fields, watching insects and collecting abandoned bird's nests. But he grew weak from the mild case of smallpox he had been given and became lonely because of his separation from his family.

Edward Jenner was born in the English town of Berkeley on May 17, 1749, the youngest of six children. His parents died within weeks of each other when he was five years old, so Edward moved in with his older brother Stephen, a clergyman.

Several years after his quarantine experience, when Edward was 13, Stephen arranged for him to become an apprentice to Daniel Ludlow, a respected country doctor who practiced medicine in the nearby town of Sodbury. Like many physicians at the time, Ludlow often traveled by horseback to see patients who were too sick to come to him. Edward Jenner was an enthusiastic student. During his seven years working with Ludlow, he learned to treat wounds, fevers, and minor diseases. Jenner also learned how to use medical equipment, including a small surgical knife known as a lancet.

One of Jenner's most memorable patients was a farm worker who said she could never catch smallpox because she had *cowpox* when she was younger. Once you had cowpox, she said, you were immune to smallpox. Cows suffering from the disease had pustules on their udders. After milking infected cows, people would get burn-like lesions on their hands and arms, and they sometimes experienced headaches and vomiting. But unlike smallpox, cowpox was never fatal, and the symptoms usually disappeared within four days. (Other animals, including horses and sheep, also suffered from similar diseases.)

Despite the woman's observation that people who had cowpox were immune to smallpox, Ludlow

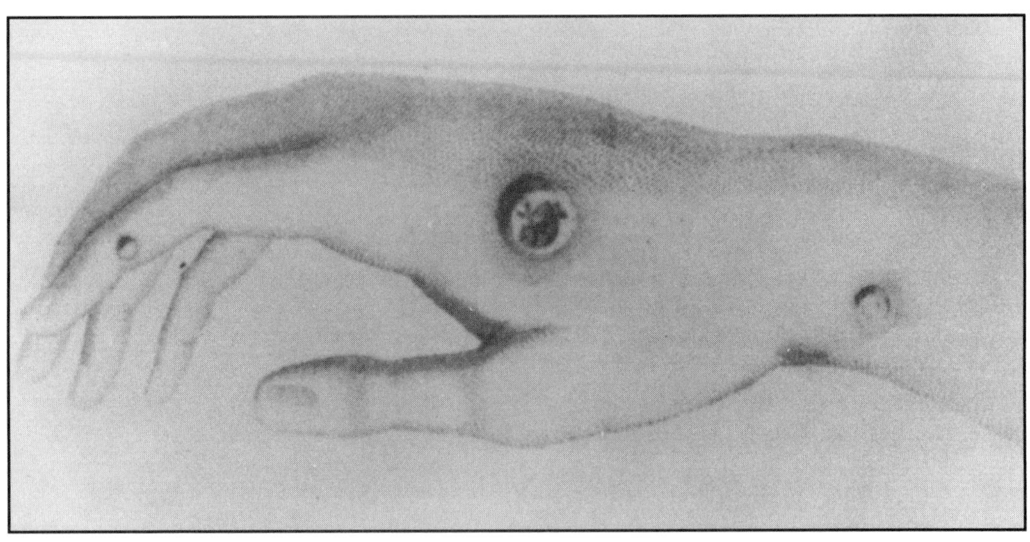

Detail of a hand with smallpox pustules

dismissed her claims as nonsense. After all, he had treated patients for smallpox who had already had cowpox. This woman's statement, however, piqued the interest of young Jenner and he never forgot it.

At age 21, Jenner finished his apprenticeship with Ludlow and decided to further his medical training by working for a city hospital. Jenner became one the first students to work under London physician John Hunter, a surgeon at St. George's Hospital who would later become famous for his research in human anatomy. The two men became good friends, and Hunter taught Jenner to take nothing for granted. The key to science, Hunter declared, was constant experimentation and the questioning of accepted facts. Jenner took this lesson to heart.

After working with Hunter for two years, Jenner returned to Berkeley in 1773 to set up his own medical practice and soon earned a reputation as a knowledgeable and talented doctor. In his spare time, he would go out into the nearby fields and observe animals, taking careful notes of what he saw. Jenner was especially interested in cuckoo birds, and his 1788 article, "Observations on the Natural History of the Cuckoo," appeared in *The Philosophical Transactions*, a prestigious journal published by the Royal Society, Britain's oldest scientific association. That year, Jenner also married a wealthy woman named Catherine Kingscote, and the couple later had two sons and a daughter.

All the while, Jenner never forgot the story he had heard about the natural protection that cowpox offered against smallpox, and now he decided to investigate that claim. Because cowpox was not a dangerous disease, no one else had taken the time to study it scientifically. Furthermore, because farms were becoming more sanitary, cowpox was becoming less common, which made it difficult for Jenner to find any outbreaks of cowpox to study. His wife, Catherine, once said she almost hoped more cows would get sick with the disease. Despite these obstacles, Jenner continued to investigate cowpox whenever a case appeared, and he eventually became an expert on the subject.

THE BREAKTHROUGH

Edward Jenner spent so much time seeking out cowpox subjects that some farmers grew tired of his constant questions about those who had contracted the disease. Although his family and friends encouraged Jenner in his research, other doctors ridiculed him, pointing out that they had known patients with smallpox who had already had cowpox. How could Jenner account for these patients? Using cowpox to defend against smallpox was a fantasy, they said. Jenner, however, remembering the miserable experience of being inoculated as a child, held onto the hope that there might be a better way to prevent the disease.

No one in the 1700s knew exactly why inoculation worked. Scientists were not aware of how white blood cells function in the human body. White blood cells scout out infections in the bloodstream—"marked" as diseases with a substance known as antigens—and then try to destroy them by releasing antitoxins, which kill the invading diseases. With some diseases, including smallpox, the body can learn to fight the infection and never catch it more than once. Other diseases, such as the common cold, are caused by so many different kinds of viruses that the body can never learn how to fight them all, and people may catch the same disease many times during their lives.

antigen: a substance or organism that causes the body to produce an antibody

antitoxin: a drug or other substance that prevents or limits the effect of a certain toxin, or poison

antibody: a substance produced by the body to destroy, weaken, or neutralize an antigen

After studying cowpox for several years, Jenner eventually came to an important conclusion. He noticed that the appearance of the pustules caused by cowpox varied from case to case. Jenner kept careful medical notes about the farm workers who had caught each type of cowpox and which of them later caught smallpox. He realized that at least two distinct types of cowpox existed, but only one special variety of the disease provided immunity from smallpox.

Jenner decided that the best way to prove his theory was to inoculate someone with that special type of cowpox. Once the patient had recovered from the virus, Jenner would then inoculate the patient with smallpox to see if he or she would catch the disease. If the patient did not contract even a mild form of smallpox during the second inoculation, then he or she had probably become immune to the disease because of the cowpox virus.

In May 1796, Jenner got the chance to test his theory when cowpox broke out on a local farm. A farm worker named Sarah Nelmes had recently caught cowpox after milking a cow. For a subject to inoculate, Jenner selected James Phipps, a healthy eight-year-old boy who had never been inoculated for smallpox. Jenner discussed his plans with James's parents, and they agreed to have their son participate in the experiment.

On May 14, Jenner scratched a pustule on Nelmes's hand with a lancet, getting some of the pus on the knife. Then he scratched James's arm to expose him to the virus. In one week, James developed the cowpox pustules, along with a slight fever and a headache. The symptoms disappeared after a few days, but Jenner decided to wait a few more

This illustration entitled "The First Vaccination" depicts Dr. Edward Jenner vaccinating James Phipps in 1796. The woman bandaging her hand is dairymaid Sarah Nelmes, who had cowpox. Jenner used pus from her infected hand for the inoculation.

weeks to make absolutely sure that the boy had returned to good health.

By July 1, Jenner was certain that James had recovered from cowpox. He scratched some smallpox pus into James's arm and waited. The incubation period for smallpox is about two weeks. Jenner was elated when three weeks passed and the boy still showed no signs of the disease.

incubation: the period between the infection by microorganisms such as bacteria or viruses and the time when symptoms begin to appear

Jenner was sure that his theory about cowpox was correct, but he knew that much work lay ahead. No one would trust his theory if he had only one successful trial. Other doctors would argue that the boy had a natural resistance to smallpox. Jenner had to test many subjects before he could present his findings to the world.

Over the next two years, Jenner inoculated nearly 25 people with the special strain of cowpox virus before writing his first book, *An Inquiry into the Causes and Effects of the Variolae Vaccinae, a Disease Discovered in Some of the Western Counties of England, Particularly Gloucestershire, and Known by the Name of Cowpox.* The book introduced the world to inoculation with cowpox.

Despite his success, Jenner never understood exactly why vaccinations worked. He did not know that white blood cells produced antitoxins to kill invading diseases. He did not understand that the special type of cowpox was so genetically similar to smallpox that the white blood cells learned to fight smallpox after being exposed to cowpox. Jenner did, however, trust his powers of observation and the results of his diligent experiments.

The smallpox inoculation was eventually dubbed vaccination, from the Latin word *vaccinus,* which means "of cows."

THE RESULTS

Even after his book was published, there was still a great deal of resistance to Jenner's claim that he had found a safe way to prevent smallpox. Many people thought it barbaric to intentionally give someone a disease that was found in cattle. Some people even believed that if they caught cowpox, they would begin to act more like an animal. Several doctors refused to consider Jenner's conclusions because they were afraid their patients would not take them seriously if they tried using his controversial methods.

Jenner's reputation was most damaged when other physicians who decided to try vaccinating patients obtained different results. Some of these doctors selected the wrong kind of cowpox while others used unwashed lancets, contaminated from use on smallpox patients, to vaccinate healthy people with cowpox. In these cases, the patients would catch the smallpox virus from the lancet before the cowpox vaccination could take effect.

By the early 1800s, however, enough British doctors had followed Jenner's vaccination techniques correctly to realize that he had, in fact, found a way to prevent smallpox. Soon, Jenner became famous throughout Europe and North America, and he eventually came to think of himself as "vaccine clerk to the world." He received thousands of letters requesting information about vaccinations and continued to give free vaccinations, knowing that to eliminate the disease entirely, vaccinations could not be withheld from those who could not afford to pay for the procedure. Other physicians, including Henry Cline, William Woodville, and George Pearson, helped to promote smallpox vaccinations throughout Britain.

Twelve thousand British subjects were vaccinated for smallpox in 1804. Although the country had been losing approximately 2,000 people each year to the disease, only 600 people died from smallpox that year. Because Jenner had devoted so much of his free time to finding a cure for smallpox when he could have been earning more money by treating patients, the British Parliament rewarded him with the sum of 20,000 British pounds, which was worth roughly $100,000 at the time.

Smallpox killed thousands of American Indians. In 1807, the chiefs of five tribes—the Mohawk, Onondaga, Seneca, Oneida, and Cayuga—showed their gratitude to Edward Jenner for his smallpox vaccine by sending him a wampum belt, decorated with polished beads. He valued this gift highly and wore the belt on special occasions.

United States president Thomas Jefferson (1743-1826) became one of Edward Jenner's biggest supporters, and the president personally vaccinated his family and about 200 other individuals.

Napoleon Bonaparte (1769-1821), the emperor of France, released two of Edward Jenner's friends from prison in 1805 in a gesture of gratitude to Jenner and his discovery.

Although his energy level declined during his sixties, Jenner remained one of Britain's most respected physicians. In 1813, Oxford University gave him an honorary doctor of medicine degree. Eight years later, he was appointed physician extraordinary to King George IV. After suffering from poor health for several years, Jenner died on January 26, 1823, at the age of 73. He was buried in the vault of Berkeley Church, next to his wife, Catherine, who had died of tuberculosis in 1815.

Over the next 150 years, smallpox vaccinations underwent only minor changes. Although they reduced the spread of the disease, smallpox was still common in many parts of the world during much of the twentieth century. Doctors learned that even though most people who caught smallpox only passed it on to one or two other people, the disease was still a dangerous one. Because small skin particles that had rubbed off, for instance, on an article of clothing could stay infected with the virus for up to 18 months, medical officials did not consider a region disease-free unless no cases were reported for two years.

In 1967, the World Health Organization (WHO) created a unit to vaccinate people and eradicate the smallpox virus world wide. That year, 44 countries reported a total of 131,418 smallpox cases, most of which occurred in India, Pakistan, Bangladesh, Brazil, and the nations of southern Africa.

In October 1979, the WHO declared that smallpox, one of the deadliest diseases in history, had been completely eradicated. Today, the virus is preserved solely for study in medical laboratories and the only reported cases after 1977 were of two laboratory scientists who had been studying the disease. After nearly two centuries, Jenner's dream of eliminating smallpox had come true.

Although Edward Jenner is now best known as the man who found the cure for smallpox, he was also responsible for making another important contribution to science. His innovative work in the late 1700s helped to set the stage for the next generation of scientific thinkers who believed in the value of experimentation and were not afraid to try new techniques to solve old problems.

The World Health Organization's extensive vaccination project in the 1960s virtually eliminated smallpox.

CHAPTER THREE

Louis Pasteur and Germ Theory

During his lifetime, Louis Pasteur changed the fields of biology, chemistry, and medicine. Yet, as a child, he was a below-average student. By the time Louis was 13, his teachers could see that he was an excellent artist. But they marked his chemistry papers "fair" or "mediocre." No one would have predicted that he would go on to change the way that scientists fought disease.

Pasteur was born near Dijon, France, on December 27, 1822. His father, Jean-Joseph Pasteur, was a tanner (someone who makes leather from animal skins). Louis's grandfather and great grandfather had also been tanners. Because tanning was such hard, messy, smelly work, Louis's parents did not want him to follow the family tradition. They made sure their son received the best education possible so that he could pursue any profession that he wanted. Jean-Joseph hoped that one day Louis would become a teacher.

Louis Pasteur (1822-1895) advised scientists and doctors to "Find the germ. Then turn it into a vaccine for the patient."

Although Louis was eager to do his best and always studied hard, he seemed to learn at a slower pace than many of his classmates. When he was fifteen, the headmaster at his school noticed that the young student's work pace was slow because he always thought problems through completely and accurately. Recognizing Louis's potential, the headmaster encouraged him to study for the entrance examinations for the École normale supérieure, the national school that trained students to be college professors.

Pasteur continued his studies at the Collège d'Arbois and Collège Royal de Besançon, both near his home. Then, in 1842, he went to Paris to study at another college, the Pension Barbet, for the entrance exam to École normale. During this time, he blossomed as a student and won awards for his scholastic achievements. He also became interested in science and mathematics and had the opportunity to attend lectures by the famous chemist Jean-Baptiste Dumas, who inspired Pasteur to concentrate his studies on chemistry.

By 1843, Pasteur had become a top student and placed fourth on the entrance exam to the École normale. For the next four years, he worked diligently, spending every spare moment in the chemistry laboratory. In 1847, the school granted him a doctor of science degree. Now Pasteur was ready to begin his career as a chemist.

From the beginning of his career, Pasteur astounded other scientists with his research abilities. For two years, he worked as a research assistant and

Jean-Baptiste Dumas (1800-1884) was the first French chemistry professor to offer laboratory instruction. He inspired one of his pupils, Louis Pasteur, to study chemistry. The American science author Isaac Asimov wrote "Although Dumas was an important scientist, Pasteur was to be a far greater one, and nothing in Dumas's scientific life was more important than the setting of Pasteur's feet on the proper road."

then won an appointment as a professor of chemistry at Strasbourg University in France.

There, Pasteur met Marie Laurent, the daughter of the university's rector. He proposed two weeks later, and they married on May 29, 1849. Laurent knew that she was marrying someone who was completely dedicated to his work, for Pasteur was usually up at dawn to get to the laboratory early, and he often stayed late. Still, he and his wife were deeply in love, and their marriage was a happy one. They had four daughters and one son. Sadly, only the son, Jean-Baptiste, and one daughter, Marie-Louise, survived to adulthood. The other three daughters died young from different illnesses. (Before the seventeenth century, three of four children died in infancy. Even as late as 1900, 30% of American children died before adolescence.)

Pasteur spent the first 10 years of his career working in the field of crystallography (the study of substances in a crystallized form). In 1854, he became dean of the Faculty of Science at Lille. During a speech to the public about the value of scientific study, Pasteur said that science awakens in humans the hope that they can solve even the worst of life's problems. He admitted that knowing when a breakthrough would happen was impossible and that luck played a big part of science. Therefore, he said, good scientists had to keep their eyes open at all times. "In the field of observation," Pasteur concluded, "chance favors only the mind which is prepared."

During Pasteur's lifetime, one of the biggest controversies in science dealt with the origins of life. Many scientists thought that microbes (living organisms too small to be seen without a microscope) were created by spontaneous generation. That is, microbes just appeared suddenly out of thin air.

At the time, people did not realize that air carried microbes. People did know, however, that boiling liquid killed these tiny organisms. Using this knowledge, several scientists conducted an experiment in which they filled a container with fluid and boiled the liquid long enough to kill all of the microbes. Then they let the container cool, leaving the top open and exposed to the air. Within a few days, the fluid would again be teeming with microscopic life. Their explanation was that this new life was formed by spontaneous generation. They did not realize that the air was carrying new microbes into the fluid.

spontaneous generation: a theory that microscopic living organisms such as bacteria simply appear. Until Louis Pasteur proved that these microbes travel through the air, many scientists believed this theory.

For thousands of years before Pasteur, people had believed this theory. For instance, because they could not see what was really happening, people thought that maggots simply appeared in old meat. In 1668, however, a scientist named Francesco Redi disproved this. Noticing that old meat always attracted flies, he wondered if some connection existed between the flies and the maggots. Redi tried to prove this connection by putting a piece of meat in a jar. Then he covered the top of the jar with gauze so air could get in but flies could not. When no maggots emerged from the meat, he knew that maggots did not simply appear, but instead came from eggs laid by the flies. Most scientists, however, ignored his results and continued to believe in spontaneous generation for another 200 years.

By the late 1800s, Pasteur and many other scientists no longer believed in spontaneous generation, although some still did. Both sides performed many experiments to prove their theories, but it was Pasteur who conducted the experiment that would eventually settle the argument.

Pasteur filled a flask, shaped like the letter S, with an organic solution. He then boiled the fluid to kill all of the microbes. Next, he waited. Because air could get into a straight-necked container, microbes

In his laboratory, Louis Pasteur devised an experiment that proved the existence of microbes in the air. This conclusion enabled him, and later other scientists, to find the cause of a disease—often the necessary first step toward a cure.

could enter and live in the fluid. But the curved neck of Pasteur's flask trapped the airborne microbes on the sides of the flask. Thus, even after many months, no microbes appeared in the liquid.

To prove his point, Pasteur took the flask and tilted it so that the fluid inside came into contact with the sides of the curved neck. Within a few days, the fluid clouded up as the microbes began multiplying.

With this experiment, Pasteur proved that the air was full of tiny microbes, too small for the human eye to see. From this, Pasteur concluded that germs floating through the air could spread contagious diseases. Before he could test his theories on disease, however, his country called on him to help avoid disaster in two of its most important industries: wine making and silk production.

France had long been famous for its wine. In the mid-1800s, however, the wine industry was in trouble. Despite the best efforts of its winemakers, more and more French wine was sour and undrinkable. No one knew why this was happening or how to prevent it. Pasteur was known for conducting laboratory studies on fermentation, the chemical reaction that turns sugar into alcohol. In July 1863, the French emperor Napoleon III asked Pasteur to study the problem.

Pasteur began his work by comparing under a microscope some sour wine with some good wine. He discovered that the sour wine was full of tiny organisms, *Mycoderma aceti*, which were used in the manufacture of vinegar. Kill these organisms,

Pasteur reasoned, and the wine should return to its normal taste.

Pasteur first tried to neutralize the acid caused by these organisms with alkali, a substance that reacts with an acid to form a salt, but this affected the taste of the wine. Next, he heated the wine briefly to between 131 and 158 degrees Fahrenheit (55 degrees celsius) and discovered that the heat destroyed the *Mycoderma aceti* but left the taste of the wine intact. The procedure had to be done when the wine was bottled, which sealed the wine from further contact with the air. His discovery saved the French wine industry.

pasteurization: the procedure of killing invading microorganisms through heating many products, including milk, wine, and beer; named for its inventor, Louis Pasteur

The French have tended their grape vineyards and made wine for centuries. Winemakers were horrified at the thought of their fine vintages being heated, but Louis Pasteur proved to them that his pasteurization process did not hurt the wine and prevented it from going sour.

While working on the wine problem, Pasteur received an urgent appeal from Jean-Baptiste Dumas, now serving as the French minister of agriculture. His old friend and former teacher wanted him to look at a disease spreading among the silkworms in France. Silkworms are caterpillars that make silk to weave cocoons. The disease that afflicted the silkworms was called pebrine, meaning "pepper disease," because the sick silkworms became spotted. It killed the silkworm eggs, worms, chrysalides, and moths and threatened the entire silk industry in France.

Reluctant to take on this task, Pasteur wrote to Dumas, "Consider, I pray you, that I have never even touched a silkworm." Dumas replied, "So much the better! For ideas you have will come to you as a result of your own observations."

Indeed, with the microscope as his greatest tool, Pasteur soon discovered that *two* separate diseases, pebrine and flacherie, were afflicting the silkworms. He showed the silkworm farmers how to recognize the diseases by using a microscope. Pebrine could be controlled by destroying diseased eggs, and flacherie could be prevented by creating larger, cleaner living conditions for the silkworms.

By 1868, Louis Pasteur had proven the germ theory and had saved two industries important to France. Had he died from the stroke he suffered that year at the age of 46, he still would have been remembered as a great scientist. But he recovered slowly and returned to his laboratory, where one of his greatest accomplishments still lay ahead.

THE BREAKTHROUGH

Pasteur once told Napoleon III that his greatest ambition was to find a way to defeat infectious disease. This desire may have come from losing three daughters to diseases when they were still young. Also, during the Franco-Prussian War (1870-1871), he had been distressed about soldiers whose wounds had become infected. Ending this suffering caused by infectious diseases became his goal.

While working on a disease in animals, Pasteur made his final great discovery. Chicken cholera was killing farmers' chickens throughout the French countryside. To discover how the disease spread, Pasteur injected chickens with the cholera virus, which he had cultivated artificially in cultures, small dishes that allowed the microorganisms to grow in the laboratory.

Pasteur began working on these experiments during the summer of 1879 before he went on vacation. After returning several weeks later, he continued his experiments where he had left off. First, he injected some chickens with the virus that he had prepared several weeks earlier. Surprisingly, none of the chickens contracted cholera from the injections. Disappointed, Pasteur was ready to start all over again when an idea struck him. What would happen, he wondered, if he were to inject these same chickens with a new batch of the cholera virus?

He prepared new cultures of the virus and injected the chickens. None of the chickens caught the disease. Pasteur realized that when the virus became old, it lost its power to make people and animals sick. In other words, it became attenuated, or weakened. The attenuated virus, however, still offered the body a chance to learn how to fight the disease and not catch it again. This process was like Edward Jenner's discovery—that cowpox teaches a body how to fight smallpox. In the old cholera virus, Pasteur had found an attenuated virus.

attenuated virus: a virus that has been weakened and made less dangerous

He then used this knowledge to fight anthrax, a fatal, contagious disease that mostly affected sheep and cattle. In 1881, he performed large-scale experiments and proved that he could weaken the anthrax virus and vaccinate cattle and sheep to protect them from the disease. Within a few years, the vaccine had spared the lives of thousands of animals and saved many farmers from economic hardship.

Having succeeded in conquering two diseases that affect animals, Pasteur now decided to dedicate his time to human diseases. "Look for the germ" became his motto whenever someone came to him for advice on how to fight a disease.

One disease that caught his attention was rabies, or hydrophobia. Rabies is spread through the saliva of already infected, or rabid, animals. Several weeks after a rabid animal bites a human being, that person develops symptoms of fever, anxiety, hyperactivity, and intense thirst, coupled with the inability to swallow. Death follows several days later.

In the 1880s, the only available treatment for rabies was burning the bite wound as soon as possible with red hot metal, a process called cauterization, in the hope of stopping the disease at its source.

Louis Pasteur shown with some of his colleagues around 1890, including (seated, left to right) Charles Louis Alphonse Laveran, Pasteur, Pierre Roux, Elie Metchnikoff, and Alexander Yersin. Laveran and Metchnikoff won Nobel Prizes in medicine in 1907 and 1908, respectively.

Pasteur remembered seeing people undergo this painful and often unsuccessful treatment when he was a child. These memories probably influenced his decision to study rabies.

Pasteur first began to work with rabid dogs and rabbits. Because rabies eventually paralyzes its victim, Pasteur decided that the best source of the virus must be in the nervous system: the brain and the spinal cord. Therefore, he removed the spinal cords from infected rabbits and kept them in tubes that were sterilized (free from germs). Then he experimented to see how much time passed before the virus weakened to the point that it would no longer kill an animal it had infected. He found that it took 14 days for the virus to become harmless.

For two weeks, Pasteur experimented with a series of rabies vaccinations in a healthy dog. On the first day, he injected the dog with a virus that had been weakened for 14 days. On the next day, he injected the dog with a virus that had been weakened for 13 days. He continued that procedure every day for 14 days. At the end of the treatment, Pasteur could inject the dog with a fresh rabies virus without the dog suffering from any symptoms. Next, he tried the technique on several dogs. The experiment was a complete success. He had proved that he could successfully vaccinate dogs against rabies.

Pasteur was not finished, however. While he could protect dogs from catching rabies, he did not know if he could cure a dog from rabies after it had been bitten. He realized that the rabies vaccine would be far more helpful if doctors could use it to treat people who already had the disease. The incubation period, the time before symptoms appear, was especially long for rabies: from two to eight weeks. Pasteur thought that this long incubation period might mean he could vaccinate a dog after it had been bitten by a rabid animal.

In the next part of his experiment, Pasteur allowed a rabid dog to bite a healthy dog. The next day, he began his vaccination treatment. Again, the experiment was a success. The dog did not contract rabies.

Pasteur successfully tried the vaccination in many more dogs, but he still hesitated to risk the life of a human being to prove that his vaccination worked. He finally decided to risk his own life by injecting himself with the rabies virus and then vaccinating himself.

Before he could begin experimenting on himself, however, an emergency arose that took the decision out of Pasteur's hands. On July 6, 1885, a frantic mother brought her nine-year-old son to Pasteur. A rabid dog had attacked and viciously bitten the boy 14 times. Joseph Meister's mother had heard about Pasteur's work with rabies, and she was desperate for his help. Pasteur could not refuse.

Pasteur began vaccinating Joseph immediately. First, he injected the child with the 14-day-old virus. Twenty-four hours later, he injected him with the 13-day-old virus. Pasteur continued this process for 14 days. Then he injected Joseph with the full-strength rabies virus. Because he was so worried about Joseph, Pasteur could barely sleep. The weeks passed slowly, but Joseph showed no signs of rabies.

When eight weeks had finally passed and the young boy was still healthy, Pasteur knew that he had discovered the cure for rabies in humans. Word spread quickly, and Pasteur soon saved another boy named Jean-Baptiste Jupille who had been bitten while beating back a rabid dog that had attacked him and five other boys. Next, a group of 19 Russians who had been attacked by a pack of rabid wolves came to France by train for treatment. Pasteur was able to save all but three of them.

The key to the treatment was administering the vaccination as soon as possible after a rabid dog had bitten a person. One time, a 10-year-old girl who had been bitten by a rabid dog 37 days earlier was brought to Pasteur. He tried to treat her, but too much time had passed. The girl soon died, which deeply saddened Pasteur.

Pasteur's mind raced with possibilities. Since he could weaken the rabies virus, perhaps scientists could control all viruses the same way. The famous French researcher pictured a world in which all contagious diseases had been wiped out and people were rarely ill.

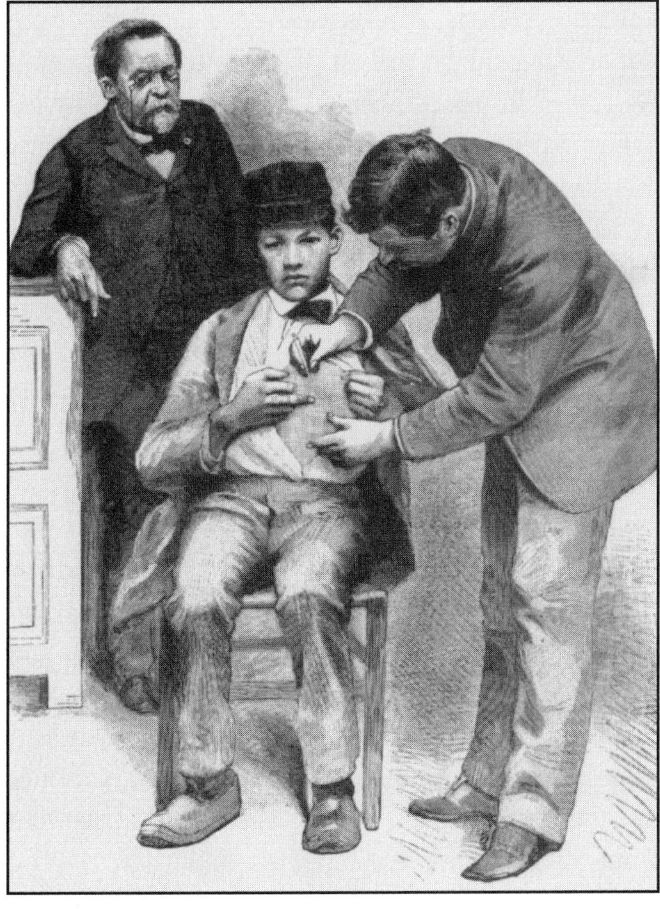

Bitten while protecting several children from a rabid dog, Jean-Baptiste Jupille (seated) was then himself saved by the new cure for rabies. Jupille, 15 years old at the time, was the second human treated with the vaccine, thanks to the work of Louis Pasteur (observing at left).

THE RESULTS

In honor of his achievements, governments and private citizens all over the world gave money to build the Pasteur Institute, which opened in Paris on November 14, 1888. This facility, the most modern in the world, was dedicated to the research of infectious diseases. Over the next century, more than 60 Pasteur Institutes would be built all over the world.

Pasteur spent the last few years of his life conducting and overseeing research at the Pasteur Institute in Paris. He also spent a great deal of time supervising the treatment of rabies patients. Every morning, he made hospital rounds to see how his rabies patients were doing, especially the children. He often corresponded with children who had been cured of rabies, including his first patient, Joseph Meister.

Engraved in marble on the walls surrounding the tomb of Louis Pasteur are the names of all of the innovations he made in science and agriculture: molecular asymmetry, fermentation, spontaneous generation, studies of wine and beer and silkworms, causes of contagious diseases, curative vaccines, and a treatment for rabies.

Louis Pasteur died on September 28, 1895, surrounded by his family and several of his colleagues. His family buried him in an ornate chapel at the Pasteur Institute in Paris.

After Pasteur's discovery of the attenuated virus, scientists from many different countries attempted to conquer infectious diseases using this method. Before the turn of the century, they had developed vaccines for typhoid fever, cholera, and the plague. In the next century, vaccines for such killers as diphtheria, tetanus, influenza, polio, measles, and mumps would follow. Some vaccines used weakened viruses; others used viruses that were not only weakened but actually killed.

Pasteur influenced medicine in other ways as well. When the English surgeon Joseph Lister read about Pasteur's germ theory in 1865, he began sterilizing wounds and surgical instruments to prevent germs from spreading from one patient to another. Before Lister, people often thought that hospitals were places to die because so many patients did die there. Between 1865 and 1869, however, the mortality rates in Lister's hospital ward dropped from 45 percent to 15 percent. During his lifetime, Lister became one of the most famous medical practitioners in the world. More than any other person, he made surgery safer for patients.

A century after Pasteur's discoveries, there are still many contagious diseases in the world. Some viruses are difficult to weaken; others are too dangerous to use even when weakened. Work goes on, however, and new innovations take place all the time. Scientists continue their efforts so that Pasteur's dream may someday finally come true.

Louis Pasteur's germ theory influenced English surgeon Joseph Lister (1827-1912), who introduced the principle of antisepsis to surgery—cleaning wounds and sterilizing tools. Lister also developed absorbable stitches and the drainage tube, both still in general use for wounds and incisions.

CHAPTER FOUR

Paul Ehrlich and Chemotherapy

In glass or plastic containers such as test tubes and petri dishes, most microorganisms are fairly easy to kill. For example, a scientist can kill *Treponema pallidum*, the organism that causes the deadly disease syphilis, with arsenic, a deadly poison. Treating a syphilitic patient with arsenic, however, would kill not only the disease but the patient as well.

Paul Ehrlich, a scientist of the late nineteenth and early twentieth centuries, wondered if he could create drugs that would target invading microorganisms while not harming the body. He spent many years of his career trying to find one of these "magic bullets" with which to treat syphilis. In fact, he tried 606 different experiments before finding a cure. This process of targeting viruses with drugs became known as chemotherapy. Although now chemotherapy is most often associated with the treatment of cancer, the term means using chemicals to treat any type of disease.

chemotherapy: the treatment of disease using chemical agents or drugs that are selectively destructive to the cause of the disease. In the 1900s, this term became most closely associated with the treatment of cancer. Chemotherapy is one of three basic ways doctors fight this disease; radiation and surgery are the other two treatments.

Scientist Paul Ehrlich (1854-1915) searched for seven years for what he called a "magic bullet" to cure syphilis.

On March 14, 1854, Paul Ehrlich was born in Strehlen, Silesia (now Strzelin, Poland). He was the only son among the five children of Jewish parents, Ismar and Rosa Ehrlich. Rosa and Ismar made a good living running a small inn called the Tavern of the Wreath of Rue. As a schoolchild, young Ehrlich excelled in Latin and math, but he did poorly in his writing classes. Later in his career, however, he learned to write clear and precise scientific papers.

When Ehrlich was a teenager, his older cousin, Carl Weigert, showed him how to stain cells with colored dyes. This process made it easier to see the different parts of the cell under a microscope. Invented by Joseph von Gerlach in 1854, this technique fascinated Ehrlich so much that he devoted his college years to the study of cells.

In fact, Ehrlich's college instructors worried that he was spending so much time with cells that he was ignoring other important subjects in his studies to become a doctor. Ehrlich had a gift for science and always got excellent grades on his tests—even though he rarely attended some of his classes.

While in college, Ehrlich met Robert Koch, an important scientist. Koch is remembered for creating guidelines for microbiologists. He established simple techniques for creating pure cultures of bacteria for study under a microscope. He was also the first to establish definitively that every contagious disease is caused by a different microorganism.

Graduating as a doctor of medicine in 1878, Ehrlich immediately found a job as an assistant to Friedrich Theodore von Frerichs. This noted

Robert Koch (1843-1910) used his own theories of bacteriology to isolate the specific bacteria in a number of diseases, including tuberculosis and cholera. He also discovered that bubonic plague was transmitted by flea-infested rats and that sleeping sickness was spread by the tsetse fly.

researcher studied liver diseases in Berlin's largest hospital, the Charité. Recognizing that 24-year-old Ehrlich was a talented researcher, the older doctor made sure that the young scientist had plenty of time to conduct his own experiments with dyes in the hospital lab. "Caged birds don't sing," Frerichs liked to say.

In 1882, Robert Koch gave a lecture on his recent discovery of the microorganism that caused tuberculosis, or TB. This deadly and contagious disease was caused by bacteria. Usually someone

---

In 1887, one of Robert Koch's assistants, Julius Richard Petri, substituted shallow glass dishes with covers for the flat glass slides that Koch was using to grow bacteria. Petri dishes have been in use ever since.

---

infected by the bacteria went months or years before the symptoms of fatigue, irritability, fever, and chills began to show. The condition worsened until the victim died. Finding the microorganism that had caused the disease was the first step to finding a cure.

Ehrlich attended Koch's lecture. Impressed by Koch's discovery, the young scientist began experimenting with dyes to see if he could improve Koch's methods. He succeeded and impressed the older scientist.

In 1887, Ehrlich made an unhappy discovery. While studying a sample of his own blood under a microscope, he saw small rods that he immediately recognized as TB. Because there was no cure for TB, the only treatment was rest and relaxation, for a well-rested body had a better chance of fighting off the disease. Paul and his wife, Hedwig, headed to southern Europe and Egypt for a two-year vacation. Fortunately, the rest allowed Ehrlich to fight off the infection with no ill effects. He returned to Germany in 1889, ready to resume his research.

By 1896, Ehrlich was known as a top scientist, and he had become the director of the new Institute for Serum Research and Serum Testing, which was located in Berlin. The building itself had once been a bakery, and later a barn, but Ehrlich did not care. He often boasted that, with some test tubes and a Bunsen burner, he could work just as well in a barn as in a laboratory.

By this time, Ehrlich was becoming legendary for his strange habits. Every night, he would write out instructions for himself and his staff on colorful note cards so that he would not forget what needed to be done the following day.

Ehrlich smoked cigars continually, often as many as two dozen a day. When visitors came to his office, he would enthusiastically tell them to have a seat. This, however, was usually quite impossible because every chair, desk, and couch would be piled high with scientific journals and many old papers. Hundreds of bottles of dyes were scattered around his office and his laboratory, most of them without labels. Even though his office appeared to be a mess, Ehrlich knew where everything was. In fact, one of his greatest fears was that someone would tidy up the place and he would not be able to find anything.

Ehrlich's trip to Egypt had interrupted his experiments with dyes. He discovered that one dye, methylene blue, was attracted to the cells of the nervous systems of rabbits. He had only mild success in using methylene blue as a pain killer, but the experiment gave him an idea.

The value of dyes to researchers was that they colored some cells but not others, such as bacteria, for example. Ehrlich reasoned a dye stain could not color a bacterium unless the stain somehow combined with that bacterium. This process usually killed the bacterium. If a dye could be found that killed a bacterium without killing other cells, it might contain a chemical that could be developed into "magic bullets" with which to target disease.

THE BREAKTHROUGH

Because he thought of himself as a detective seeking clues to scientific questions, Paul Ehrlich liked to read detective stories, especially about Sherlock Holmes. He also read numerous scientific journals. In 1901, he read an article written by Charles Louis Alphonse Laveran, the French scientist who had discovered the microorganism that causes malaria, a disease spread by mosquitoes.

In this particular article, Laveran described experiments in which he had injected mice with trypanosomes, the organism that in humans causes a disease called sleeping sickness. Trypanosomes killed every mouse that he had injected. Ehrlich thought back to his experiments with methylene blue, and wondered if he could create a dye that was attracted to trypanosomes.

In 1902, Ehrlich began the search for a drug that would cure sleeping sickness without killing the mice. His search for a drug took him seven years.

Ehrlich and his assistants tried all sorts of dyes. They had worked with some of them before; others were created for this experiment. Ehrlich's first small success came a year after the search had begun. He and his assistants injected a mouse with a dye called trypan red. To their amazement, a single injection cured the mouse. The dye, however, did not always work with mice, and it never worked in humans. Still, this small step forward encouraged Ehrlich and his assistants to press on in their search for a drug that would cure sleeping sickness. An article that

Ehrlich read in 1905 changed the direction of his research. H. Wolferstan Thomas and Anton Breinl had discovered that a chemical known as atoxyl destroyed trypanosomes. (The name "atoxyl" means "not poisonous," which is odd because the chemical contains arsenic, a highly toxic poison that could cause blindness and death. It is a drug and not a dye.) Ehrlich and his staff immediately began testing atoxyl. With each failure, they would add or subtract chemicals and try again.

The search became even more pressing in 1906 when German zoologist Fritz Schaudinn discovered the microorganism that caused syphilis. Syphilis is a sexually transmitted disease; that is, it spreads by

A syphilis patient sits in a fumigation stove while an assistant adds more fuel. This was one of many painful and unsuccessful treatments for the disease. The writing on the stove says "for one pleasure a thousand pains." Jacques Laniet Receuil engraved the picture in the 1600s.

sexual contact between people. It can remain in the body for years without any symptoms, and some people with syphilis never know they have the disease. These people, however, can spread the disease to others. People who become ill suffer skin lesions, damage to internal organs such as the heart, and progressive central nervous system damage that can lead to insanity, paralysis, blindness, and even death. The disease first appeared in Spain in 1493 among sailors who had returned from the New World, and after that date it became common, spreading to millions of people around the world.

The discovery of the syphilis bacteria was important to Ehrlich because Schaudinn thought that the syphilis bacteria and trypanosomes were closely related. Ehrlich believed that if he could find the cure for sleeping sickness, he could also cure syphilis.

One of Paul Ehrlich's assistants was the Japanese scientist Sahashiro Hata, pictured here in 1923. Hata performed Ehrlich's experiments.

By 1909, Ehrlich and his assistants had a routine. Ehrlich would provide the ideas and the leadership while his head assistant, Alfred Bertheim, would prepare each drug, adding or subtracting chemicals according to Ehrlich's instructions. Another assistant, a Japanese scientist named Sahashiro Hata, would run the experiments and report the results. Then the process would begin again.

After what Ehrlich called "seven years of misfortune," the fateful day came in June 1909 when Hata injected a syphilis-infected mouse with a drug named Preparation 606 because it was the 606th one the team had created. With a single injection, the mouse was cured, without any side effects.

As prepared by Bertheim, Preparation 606 was a combination of many fairly common chemicals, including oxygen, hydrogen, chlorine, and arsenic. Its scientific name was "Dioxy-diamino-arsenobenzol-dihydro-chloride."

Hata and Ehrlich took their experiment one step further. They injected the drug into a rabbit infected with syphilis and waited. In less than 24 hours, the infection began to clear and the rabbit was completely cured within three weeks, again with no side effects.

In September, after further successful trials with animals, Ehrlich contacted Konrad Alt, the superintendent of an insane asylum in Germany. Because syphilis often caused insanity, many of the patients in the asylum already had this disease. In several patients, paralysis was already setting in, and death was near. Although Alt believed that the disease had progressed too far in all of these patients, he agreed to try Preparation 606 on them. He was shocked when he found that a single injection of 606 cured every single patient. Ehrlich's dream of finding magic bullets had finally come true, and he had proven that diseases could be cured with chemicals. Chemotherapy was born.

THE RESULTS

Demand instantly erupted for Preparation 606, which Ehrlich named salvarsan. Doctors treated thousands of patients with salvarsan within the first year, and Ehrlich tracked and reviewed all of the cases to be sure no one suffered any severe side effects. Although clinical trials with thousands of people would eventually become common, this sort of trial was unheard of in 1909. Still, Ehrlich realized that longer trials would be necessary to find all of the potential dangers of his drug.

Paul Ehrlich distributed thousands of doses of salvarsan free of charge to doctors all around the world.

Paul Ehrlich had won the Nobel Prize in medicine in 1908, a year before the breakthrough of salvarsan. The Nobel committee had awarded Ehrlich this prize for his immunity research. The Nobel Prize, which was first given in 1901, was a very prestigious honor for any scientist. But now salvarsan brought Ehrlich even greater fame, and countries all over the world awarded him honors for his great discovery.

On August 20, 1915, at the age of 61, Paul Ehrlich died of a heart attack. His obituary in the *Times* of London best sums up the way the world regarded him: "He opened new doors to the unknown, and the whole world at this hour is his debtor."

Chemotherapy was a new weapon in the arsenals of doctors and researchers. Progress in chemotherapy, however, was slow until the mid-1930s. At that time, German researcher Gerhard Domagk developed prontosil, a chemotherapeutic drug that killed streptococci, a group of bacteria that could cause sore throats, fever, and skin infections.

The most famous chemotherapeutic drug of all would be penicillin, which Alexander Fleming would discover in 1928 and Howard Florey and Ernst Chain would develop in the 1940s. Penicillin would prove to be effective against a wide variety of diseases, including diphtheria and tetanus, as well as infections. Penicillin even replaced salvarsan as a cure for syphilis.

A growing problem in chemotherapy is that some viruses and bacteria that cause diseases are becoming immune to many drugs. Over time, these organisms mutate and change, so some diseases that were easily cured at one time have now become resistant to treatment. The challenge for scientists is either to keep one step ahead of a disease by developing new drugs or to develop completely new ways of fighting a disease.

CHAPTER FIVE

Frederick Banting and Insulin

Most medical breakthroughs are the result of a lifetime of scientific work. Edward Jenner, for example, devoted years to the pursuit of a smallpox vaccine, and Paul Ehrlich had to endure what he called "seven years of misfortune" to develop chemotherapy. Both spent their lives studying science in the hope of one day making a great discovery.

The story of Frederick Banting, however, is very different. Banting, who discovered insulin, a drug that has helped millions of people with diabetes lead full lives, was a surgeon, not a scientist. But he had an idea and the determination to see his idea through to the eventual discovery of insulin. Banting would go on to become one of the most famous medical researchers in history.

Frederick G. Banting (1891-1941), the first Canadian to win a Nobel Prize in medicine, as he looked in 1921 when he began his historic research.

Frederick Grant Banting was born in Alliston, Ontario, on November 14, 1891, the son of William and Margaret Banting. Frederick was the youngest of six children in this hard-working farming family.

Throughout his school years, Banting was shy and withdrawn, but he did fairly well in all of his subjects, except for spelling. When he went to Victoria College in 1910, he was not sure of his career path. His parents wanted him to be a Methodist minister, but Banting decided to become a doctor instead. He obtained his parents' blessing for this ambition and, in 1912, began his first year of medical school at the University of Toronto.

World War I interrupted Banting's studies in 1916. The Allies desperately needed doctors, so the university shortened the fifth and final year of medical school for his class to a single summer session. Banting and nearly all his classmates enlisted to serve as medical personnel in the Canadian military.

During World War I, Frederick Banting operated on wounded soldiers in hospitals like this one in France.

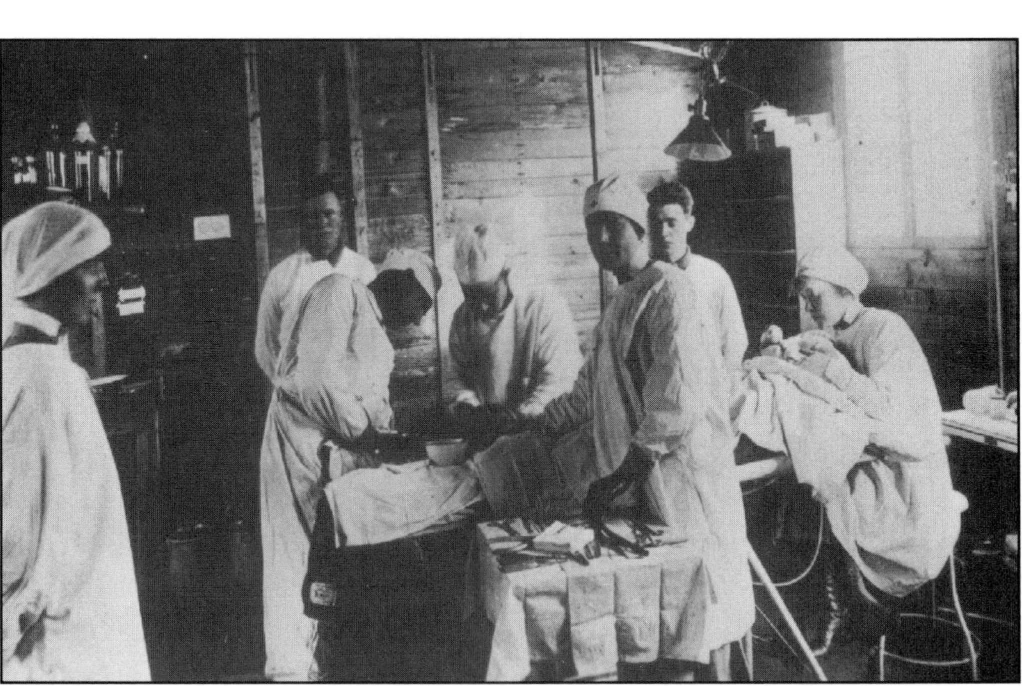

Because of the shortage of medical officers, Banting was forced to quickly learn the art of surgery, his chosen specialty. He became a skilled surgeon and spent much of his time serving near the front lines in France. A brave man, Banting often put himself in danger to help wounded soldiers on the battlefield. For his heroic services, his country awarded him the prestigious Military Cross. In 1918, a piece of shrapnel wounded Banting in his right arm, ending his army career. He spent nine weeks in an English hospital because the wound became infected, but he fortunately regained the full use of his arm.

The young doctor returned to Canada in 1919, ready to begin his medical career. For a year, he was a surgical apprentice, or intern, in Toronto. But this Canadian city was already filled with surgeons, so Banting decided to set up his own private practice in London, Ontario, a prosperous, growing community west of Toronto.

Because no one knew him in London, and because he hadn't started out practicing with an older doctor, Banting's private practice began dismally. Four agonizing weeks passed before his first patient arrived, and growth was slow after that. Frustrated, Banting earned money by teaching anatomy at the nearby University of Western Ontario.

On Monday, November 1, 1920, Banting was supposed to give a lecture about the human pancreas, an organ located below and behind the stomach. The day before the lecture, he reviewed his old textbooks and, just before going to bed that

Diabetes occurs in two forms, juvenile and adult-onset diabetes. The juvenile form begins in childhood and usually requires the use of insulin injections to control the level of sugar in the blood. The adult form may also require insulin injections, but may often be treated effectively with pills that act like insulin to lower the blood sugar level. Many of these adults may only require a change in their diet or exercise routine to control their blood sugar. Studies have shown a decrease in the complications from both forms of diabetes when blood sugar levels are closely controlled.

night, he read an article about the pancreas in a surgical journal. While reading this article, he came up with the idea that would change his life.

The pancreas helps the human body to convert food into energy. Most of the energy needed by the body comes from carbohydrates. In the human body, the carbohydrates in food break down into a simple sugar called glucose. Through a process called metabolism, the pancreas turns glucose into energy that the body can use. If the pancreas is not working correctly, the body cannot metabolize glucose or gain energy from carbohydrates. Sugar levels then begin to build in the blood. This condition is called diabetes.

People living with diabetes become increasingly hungry as the body, unable to metabolize glucose, tries to find energy. Soon they become listless and begin to lose weight as the body converts fat instead of glucose into energy. With no way to gain energy, a person with diabetes eventually goes into a coma and dies. This deadly process can take months or years, depending on the person.

Scientists began associating diabetes with the pancreas because of an accidental discovery in 1889. While experimenting on the pancreas in dogs, Oskar Minkowski and Joseph von Mering surgically removed a dog's pancreas. They were surprised to discover that the dog quickly came down with a severe case of diabetes.

Unlike smallpox or syphilis, diabetes was spread neither by viruses nor bacteria. Although researchers did not understand diabetes very well, they believed it to be a hereditary disease in humans, a disease that parents can pass on to their children. Many things—including trauma, pregnancy, and bacterial infections—can trigger diabetes in people who are born with a susceptibility to the disease.

Moses Barron, a doctor from Minneapolis, Minnesota, had written the article Banting read that momentous night before his lecture. The article was about a part of the pancreas called the islets of Langerhans, which were named after Paul Langerhans, the doctor who had discovered this special cell construction in 1869. Barron noted that if the entire pancreas had to be removed or was destroyed, his patient would come down with diabetes. If the islets were intact, however, a patient could still metabolize glucose. Thus, the islets of Langerhans had to be the key in turning glucose into energy. Although other researchers had reached the same conclusion, no one had found a way to help those who were living with diabetes.

Banting couldn't sleep that night. At some point he got up and wrote down an idea: Would it be possible to take fluid from the islets of Langerhans and inject it into a diabetic? If that were possible, those injections might allow diabetics to metabolize glucose in the normal way.

John J. R. Macleod was head of the physiology department at the University of Toronto in 1921 when a young doctor named Frederick Banting persuaded him to provide laboratory space and resources for experiments.

Quickly, Banting began to plan his experiments. He first went to the University of Toronto to seek the advice of John J. R. Macleod, an internationally recognized expert on metabolism. Banting hoped that Macleod might offer him the resources to conduct the experiments.

Macleod was blunt with Banting. Many researchers had tried this experiment before, he said, with little success. But because Banting still seemed willing to put in the time and effort, Macleod agreed to give him an assistant for two months, as well as a small research lab and ten dogs on which to experiment.

Even though far more experienced and knowledgeable researchers had failed in the past, Macleod had several reasons for agreeing to let Banting try his experiments. First of all, Banting's surgical experience would be an advantage in the tricky pancreatic operation. During this operation, the surgeon must tie off the pancreas without hurting the islets of Langerhans. The experiments of other scientists had failed because they were unable to complete this operation successfully.

Second, new techniques were available to test blood-sugar levels. One way to tell if a patient had diabetes was if there was too much sugar in the blood. The inability to measure results accurately had thwarted the past efforts of researchers.

Finally, Macleod knew that even negative results have value. Diabetes was a deadly disease, and millions of people suffered from it worldwide. Records exist that suggest people had been aware of diabetes for more than 4,000 years. For all of these reasons, Macleod encouraged Banting to go ahead.

THE BREAKTHROUGH

On May 14, 1921, Banting locked up his medical practice in London, Ontario, for the summer and left for Toronto. At the time, he did not know that he would never practice in London again. When he arrived in Toronto, Macleod introduced him to Charles Herbert Best, the graduate student in biochemistry who would be Banting's assistant.

Banting had only eight short weeks that summer to conduct his experiment, but he had already planned out his time. On May 17, he and Best removed pancreases from several dogs, knowing that these dogs would develop diabetes. He also operated on several dogs to tie off the ducts of their pancreas. Tying off the ducts that connected the pancreas to the stomach and intestine would destroy the pancreas by causing it to shrivel up, or atrophy, but the islets of Langerhans would stay healthy. Then he would treat the newly diabetic dogs with fluid extracted from the islets of Langerhans of the dogs whose pancreatic ducts had been tied off.

Several dogs died before Banting learned exactly how to perform the complicated operation. Both he and Best knew from the experiences of other researchers that they would have to wait several weeks for the pancreases to atrophy completely. When they opened up the dogs in the first week of July, however, they found that because they had not tied off the pancreas ducts tightly enough, nothing had happened. Now they had to start again with nothing to show for their efforts of the previous

Biochemist Charles Herbert Best had experience testing blood-sugar levels when he began assisting Frederick Banting with pancreas experiments in 1921.

weeks. Macleod, who had supplied the funds for the experiments, had left for vacation in the middle of June, so Banting used his own money to buy several more dogs.

By the end of July, Banting and Best were finally ready to try the next step of their experiment. They had a dog with diabetes and a dog with an atrophied pancreas. The two men removed the dog's atrophied pancreas, sliced up the organ, and chilled it in a salt solution. When they filtered the solution, they were left with the extract from the pancreas.

A normal blood-sugar level in dogs is between .08 and .13 percent. While this is a small fraction of the blood (about one-tenth of one percent), it is vital for the dogs' health. The blood-sugar level in the diabetic dog was .20 percent. An hour after the diabetic dog was injected with the solution made from the other dog's atrophied pancreas, the blood-sugar level of the diabetic dog had fallen to .12 percent. A second injection reduced it to .11 percent.

Encouraged by their results, Banting and Best began working around the clock to keep diabetic dogs alive with "isletin," the name Banting had given to the extract. They experimented with different doses of the drug, and, when they ran out of isletin, they used extract from fresh pancreases, instead of atrophied ones. Although their results showed that this extract worked as well as isletin, for unknown reasons, they missed this result. The two researchers continued to produce isletin, which is a far more complicated process than simply taking an extract from a healthy pancreas.

Charles Best (left) and Frederick Banting pose with one of the many dogs they used in their experiments.

When Macleod arrived back in Toronto on September 21, he was impressed with the two men's results. Now Macleod's experience as a researcher became invaluable. He knew that many scientists would be critical of their results, so he told Banting and Best to try their experiment many times to be positive that it worked. He also suggested new experiments, one of which proved what they had missed earlier: that an extract from the whole pancreas was as effective as isletin in treating diabetes.

In December 1921, Macleod added James Collip, an experienced biochemist, to their team.

James Collip, a gifted biochemist, purified the Banting and Best extract, producing the drug "insulin" that has saved millions of lives.

Banting and Macleod knew they would need an expert's help if they were going to make their extract pure enough for human use. Impure drugs were unpredictable, painful to take, and often caused unwanted side effects.

On January 11, 1922, the extract underwent its crucial test. Leonard Thompson, a 14-year-old boy living with diabetes, was a patient at Toronto General Hospital. Listless and semicomatose, he was losing weight quickly. Fearing for his life, his doctors permitted the researchers to administer their new drug. Nothing happened. Collip went back to the laboratory, where he successfully purified the extract. On January 23, Leonard was injected again. This time, the results were dramatic. Leonard's blood sugar dropped to normal, and he immediately began to gain strength.

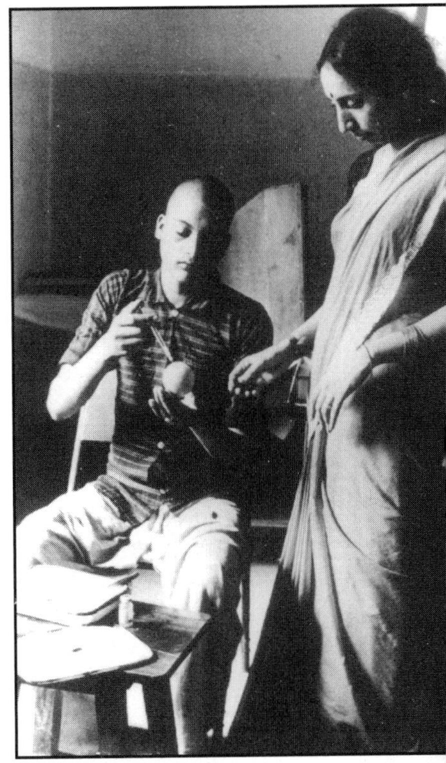

Diabetics learn how to inject themselves with insulin by practicing on an orange.

The team named the new drug "insulin." It did not cure diabetes, but regular injections allowed a human body to metabolize glucose. Eli Lilly, a pharmaceutical company in Indianapolis, Indiana, collaborated with Banting and his team to produce the large amounts of insulin that were needed by diabetics.

Frederick Banting became famous after his discovery of insulin. He even had a crater on the moon named in his honor.

THE RESULTS

Because of his inexperience, Banting was afraid that Macleod would get all of the credit for discovering insulin. Despite his worries, Banting became a hero in Canada and around the world. Newspapers headlined his name, and several universities awarded him honorary degrees. For his work, the University of Toronto gave him a gold medal and a doctor of medicine degree. (Before this, Banting had only a bachelor's degree.) The government established the Banting and Best Chair of Medical Research at the University, and granted Banting a lifetime annuity so he would be free to continue his research. In 1934, he was knighted by King George V of England, who was a diabetic.

In 1923, the Nobel committee awarded Banting the Nobel Prize in medicine. While he was pleased at winning the award, he was furious when Macleod, instead of Best, was chosen to share the honor with him. After all, Macleod was not even in the country when Banting and Best had made their discovery. To ensure that justice was done, Banting immediately split his share of the prize money with Best. Macleod followed Banting's example and split his share with Collip, the biochemist who had purified the extract.

Even though Banting and Macleod won the Nobel Prize, all four members of the team had been essential for the discovery of insulin. Banting provided the initial idea, the surgical skills, and the drive to keep going. Best provided expertise in measuring blood sugar. Collip purified the drug. Macleod had provided resources and experience.

Banting devoted the rest of his career to scientific research. Although he never made another important breakthrough, he was, according to one biographer, "idolized by his associates and by Canadians in general." As director of a research department, Banting described himself as "a catalyst which accelerates a reaction without taking part in it." He encouraged and assisted his staff and lobbied for government support for their projects.

When World War II broke out in Europe in 1939, Banting was anxious to serve his country again. Because the army considered him too valuable to risk as a surgeon on the front lines, he was assigned to coordinate research efforts between Britain and Canada. His duties required regular trips back and forth between the two countries.

On February 20, 1941, Banting was a passenger aboard a military plane headed for England. Shortly after taking off, engine failure caused the plane to lose altitude. The pilot turned the plane around, but he was unable to fly it back to the home base. Only the pilot survived the crash. All of Canada mourned the loss of its great hero.

Research on diabetes continues today, for a cure has yet to be found. Along with proper diet and exercise, however, insulin makes the disease treatable. While insulin does not work for everyone, it can help most diabetics and millions of people who would have died without the drug are now able to live normal lives with it.

In the United States alone, 10 million people have diabetes. Doctors diagnose another 500,000 new cases each year, and more than 30,000 Americans die every year from the complications of diabetes.

Frederick Banting served in the Canadian army as a surgeon during World War I and as a research coordinator during World War II. He was on a mission to England in 1941, when he was killed in a plane crash in Newfoundland.

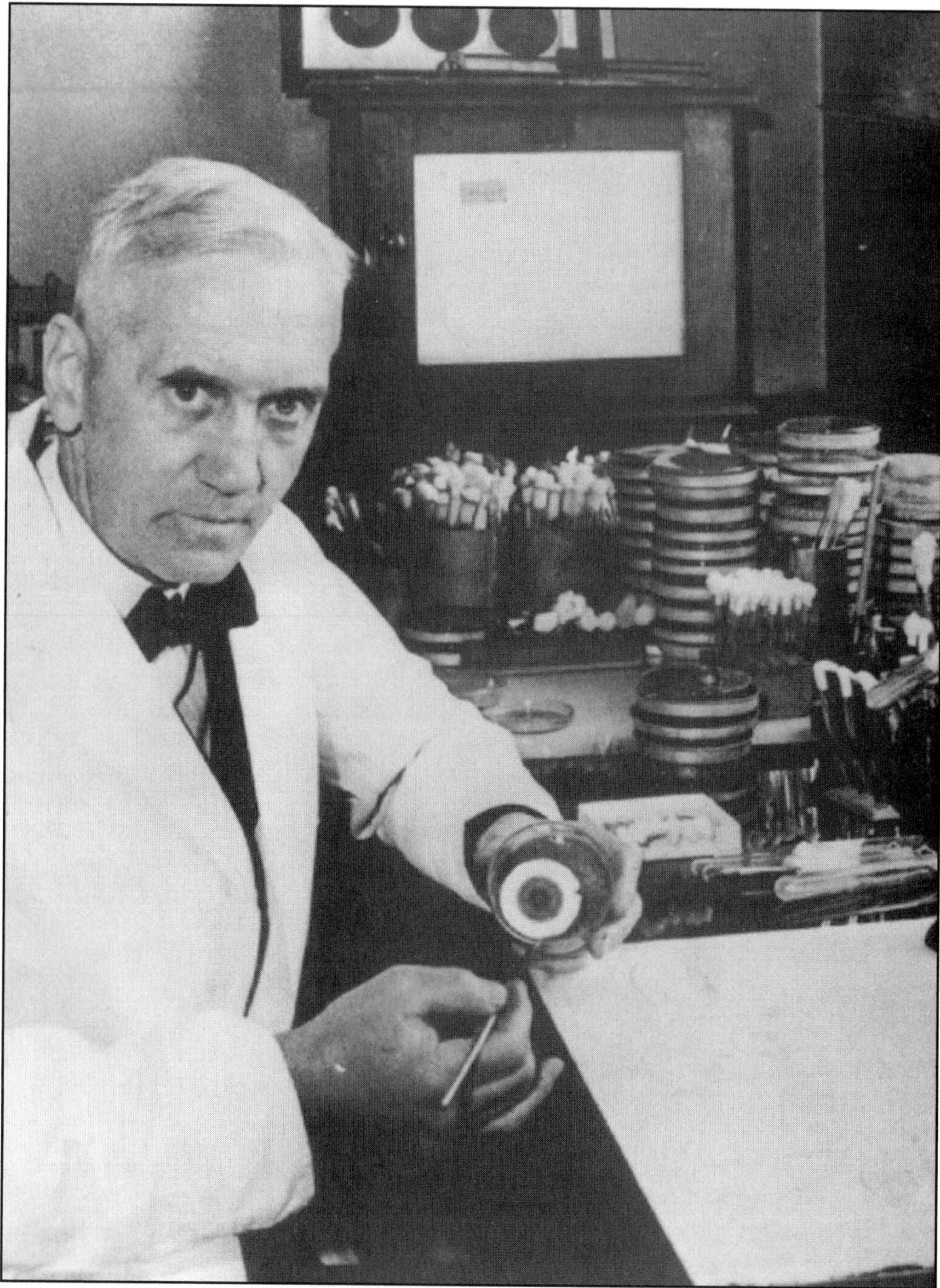

CHAPTER SIX

Alexander Fleming and Penicillin

Skin is one of the human body's best defenses against disease. Our skin keeps most bacteria, viruses, and other tiny predators from entering our bodies and making us ill. Yet even the tiniest paper cut can allow these microorganisms into our bloodstream. When bacteria multiply under the surface of the skin, a cut becomes infected. Serious infections can be life threatening, but doctors can use drugs called antibiotics to kill bacteria that have entered the body. In 1928, Alexander Fleming discovered the most important of these antibiotics: penicillin. Later, in 1940, Howard Florey and Ernst Chain turned his discovery into a drug that would help millions.

The story of penicillin begins in a remote farmhouse in Scotland on August 6, 1881, the day Alexander Fleming was born. The son of Hugh and Grace Fleming, he was the second youngest of eight children. School was easy for young Alec, so he spent little time studying. He had an incredible

A keen eye and a cluttered laboratory led Alexander Fleming (1881-1955) to a discovery that made medical history.

memory and memorized facts easily. An energetic child, Alec loved to play games. But he also could be very quiet and, as an adult, preferred silence to idle conversation.

As a teenager, Alec went to live with an older brother, Tom, in London, England. There he worked as an office clerk in a shipping firm. After receiving a small inheritance from an uncle, Alec enrolled in St. Mary's Hospital Medical School in 1901.

A top student, Fleming graduated as a qualified doctor in 1906. During his student years, he was a member of the St. Mary's Rifle Club and had become an excellent marksman. The year Fleming graduated, the team was preparing for a run at the prestigious Armitage Cup. Even though he was more interested in becoming a surgeon than a scientist, he stayed at the school an extra year as a research assistant, because the club needed his skill with a rifle.

At St. Mary's, Fleming became an assistant to Sir Almroth Wright in the Inoculation Department. Wright was famous for his work with vaccines, especially against the disease of typhoid. An exceptionally hard worker who stayed in his laboratory from early in the morning until late at night nearly every day, Wright expected the same level of commitment from his assistants. Fleming greatly respected Wright and enjoyed the research so much that he remained in the Inoculation Department for 49 years.

When World War I erupted, Fleming joined the British army and served as a medical officer in

France, where he experimented with antiseptics. While on leave in 1915, he married a nurse, Sarah McElroy, who liked to be called "Sareen." She was as outgoing as Fleming was quiet and ran a nursing home with her twin sister, Elizabeth—who later married Fleming's brother John.

After the war, Fleming worked with a chemical called lysozyme, which is found in body fluids such as mucus and tears. The young scientist discovered that this enzyme helped to keep bacteria from entering the body. His discovery helped later scientists understand how the body's immune system worked.

Fleming may also have been one of the first doctors in England to administer the drug salvarsan—the new "magic bullet" that cured syphilis. Discovered by Paul Ehrlich in 1909, Fleming was one of the few doctors skilled enough to inject salvarsan into a person's vein—a quicker and more effective method than injecting the solution into a muscle.

Fleming never kept his lab very neat. His lab bench was always scattered with specimens and cultures on which he was working. Without his messiness, however, Fleming said he would not have made his great discovery in 1928.

During that summer, Fleming was experimenting with staphylococcus, a bacterium that is dangerous to humans when it infects a wound. When he went on a vacation, Fleming had left several cultures of the bacteria growing. On his return to the lab several weeks later, Fleming found a fuzzy, blue circle of mold growing in one of the cultures.

When Fleming examined the petri dish under a microscope, he discovered that all the staphylococci surrounding the mold had died. This mold, which could kill the dreaded staphylococci bacteria, excited Fleming. He sent part of the sample to a chemist who identified the mold as a type of penicillia, similar to the kind that grows on old bread. Fleming named the extract he made from the mold penicillin.

The penicillia mold's name comes from the Latin word *penicillus,* meaning brush, which it resembles under a microscope.

Fleming's discovery was actually a stroke of luck. Scientists later discovered that penicillin does not kill fully grown bacteria. Instead, it kills them as they grow, preventing the bacteria from successfully reproducing. Fortunately, a cold snap in the weather

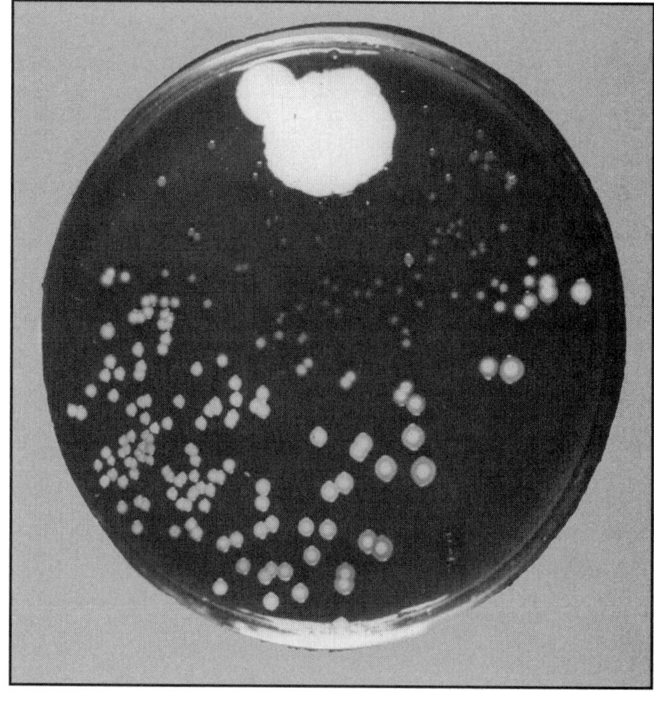

This penicillin mold grew quite by chance in 1928. But Alexander Fleming immediately recognized that it had stopped the growth of bacteria surrounding it and photographed his discovery.

had temporarily stopped the bacteria from growing. During this cold spell, a spore of penicillin mold had landed in the dish and began to grow. When the weather warmed up, the bacteria near the mold could not multiply. The occurrence was a rare one and, had Fleming not been observant, he would have missed it. But Fleming's acute power of observation was described this way: "His mind would pounce on the one odd happening that would prove to be significant." Moreover, had he kept his lab tidy and his specimens protected, the mold would never have landed in the culture.

After writing a paper describing his discovery, Fleming experimented with using penicillin to kill bacteria in infected wounds. Unfortunately, he soon learned that while it takes penicillin about four hours to kill bacteria, the human body washes penicillin from the blood stream in less than two hours. Penicillin was also difficult to work with and to purify. Eventually, Fleming gave up on penicillin and went on to other experiments. But he carefully preserved samples of penicillin for future use.

For the next 10 years, Fleming devoted no time to penicillin, although a few of his assistants tried some experiments with the mold. The significance of his earlier discovery might have been lost forever if it were not for the efforts of Howard Florey and Ernst Chain in the late 1930s.

Born on September 24, 1898, Howard Walter Florey was a native of Adelaide, Australia. Howard, the youngest child of Bertha and Joseph Florey, had four older sisters. Like Fleming, Florey was an

Alexander Fleming working at St. Mary's Hospital Medical School in 1925

outstanding student and athlete. Unlike Fleming, who, despite his shyness, was easygoing and popular, Florey was fiercely competitive and not well liked.

In December 1921, Florey left Australia to continue his medical studies at Oxford University on a Rhodes scholarship. He sailed to England as a ship's surgeon on a cargo steamer in exchange for his passage. At Oxford, Sir Charles Sherrington, a master of scientific technique who would win a Nobel Prize in 1932, was Florey's mentor. Sherrington encouraged him to study blood movement through the capillaries (tiny blood vessels in the body). From this study, Florey became interested in white blood cells and the subject of immunity.

Florey worked as a professor at Sheffield University from 1927 to 1935, when he returned to Oxford as chairman of the pathology department. There, he assembled a team of scientists to work with him. One of them, Ernst Chain, was a Jewish biochemist who had left Germany to escape the Nazis. Together, Florey and Chain turned penicillin into a wonder drug that has saved millions of lives and remains one of the most important remedies available today for curing a long list of bacteria-caused diseases.

Ernst Chain, who fled to England to escape Nazi persecution in Germany, rediscovered Fleming's paper on penicillin.

THE BREAKTHROUGH

Florey and Chain began by researching lysozyme, the enzyme that Fleming had discovered some 15 years earlier. Under Florey's direction, Chain discovered how lysozymes destroy bacteria that enter the body through the nose and the eyes. When this research was complete, Florey and Chain decided to look for other natural substances that might prevent infection. Chain collected almost 200 articles about promising research in fighting infections, including Fleming's report on penicillin. Because both men thought penicillin was worth a look, they immediately began experimenting with it.

To be sure that penicillin worked as well as Fleming had claimed, Chain did some preliminary tests on it. His results were so positive that Florey decided to devote all of the resources of the department to penicillin research. Because this was late in 1939 and Britain had just declared war on Germany, research money was scarce. So Florey turned to the Rockefeller Foundation in the United States, which granted him the money for his research.

As the first step in their work with penicillin, Florey and Chain purified the mold for testing. This was not easy to do, but with the entire research team working together, the task went quickly. By March 1940, Florey and Chain had enough penicillin to begin their experiments.

On May 25, while the British army was trapped by the Germans at Dunkirk in France, Chain and Florey injected eight mice with deadly streptococci.

Then the team of researchers injected four of the mice with penicillin. Florey and Chain thought that penicillin did not last long enough in the body to kill bacteria, so they injected more penicillin into two of the four mice every two hours. The results were spectacular. By morning, the four mice that had received one or more injections of penicillin were perfectly healthy, while the four that had not been treated were dead.

Florey and Chain were so worried about a German invasion that they smeared spores of penicillin into their coat linings. If their lab was destroyed, they hoped that one of them could escape and resume their work elsewhere.

The Germans did not invade, but without proof that the drug worked in human beings, Florey could not convince British pharmaceutical companies to begin producing penicillin. The companies were busy making drugs to help wounded soldiers and did not want to risk investing in something that might fail. Since a human being would need 3,000 times as much penicillin as a mouse, the Oxford team began making as much of the drug as possible in their own laboratory.

Production was slow. January 1941 rolled around before the team had enough penicillin to begin testing the drug on people. Florey and Chain first tried the drug on healthy volunteers to make sure it was not poisonous to humans and to determine the most effective doses. When the drug proved harmless to humans, they began searching for a patient whose life was threatened by infection.

Howard Florey, right, photographed in 1946 at the Pasteur Institute in Paris with Dr. Michel Fauguet

When viewing the results of their successful experiments treating mice with penicillin, Florey commented that penicillin ***"looks promising."*** Chain replied, ***"It's a miracle."***

On February 1, 1941, the team found Albert Alexander, a 43-year-old police officer. Two months before, Alexander had scratched his face on a rosebush thorn. The wound had become infected, and the infection had spread to his eyes, lungs, and shoulders. In fact, doctors had already removed his left eye. Alexander's life was in grave danger, but after being injected with penicillin at three-hour intervals, he improved dramatically. Within 24 hours, his appetite returned and his fever broke. A week later, he seemed to have regained his health. The team stopped his treatment and began to treat a 15-year-old boy who was dying of a streptococcal infection.

This second patient recovered within a couple of days. Unfortunately, just as the research team used up the last of its penicillin, they discovered that they had not treated their first patient long enough to kill all of his infection. Alexander suffered a relapse and died a few weeks later.

Confident that more penicillin would have saved Alexander, Florey and Chain produced a greater quantity of the drug and tested it on several more patients, all with positive results. Seventeen people had to work seven days a week for several months to produce enough penicillin to treat six patients for a few days each. But, finally, they had developed a drug that would cure infections and save thousands of lives every year.

THE RESULTS

With the potential of penicillin no longer in doubt, several U.S. pharmaceutical companies began to produce the drug. The United States was about to enter World War II, and these companies thought that penicillin would be the ideal drug to save the lives of wounded American soldiers. Penicillin proved to be difficult to work with, however, and three years passed before the companies were able to mass-produce it. But by June 1944, the drug companies had enough penicillin available to treat all of the casualties from the Allied invasion of Europe.

When U.S. general Dwight Eisenhower gave the order to begin the Allied invasion of Nazi-occupied France on June 6, 1944, enough penicillin was available to treat all of the wounded.

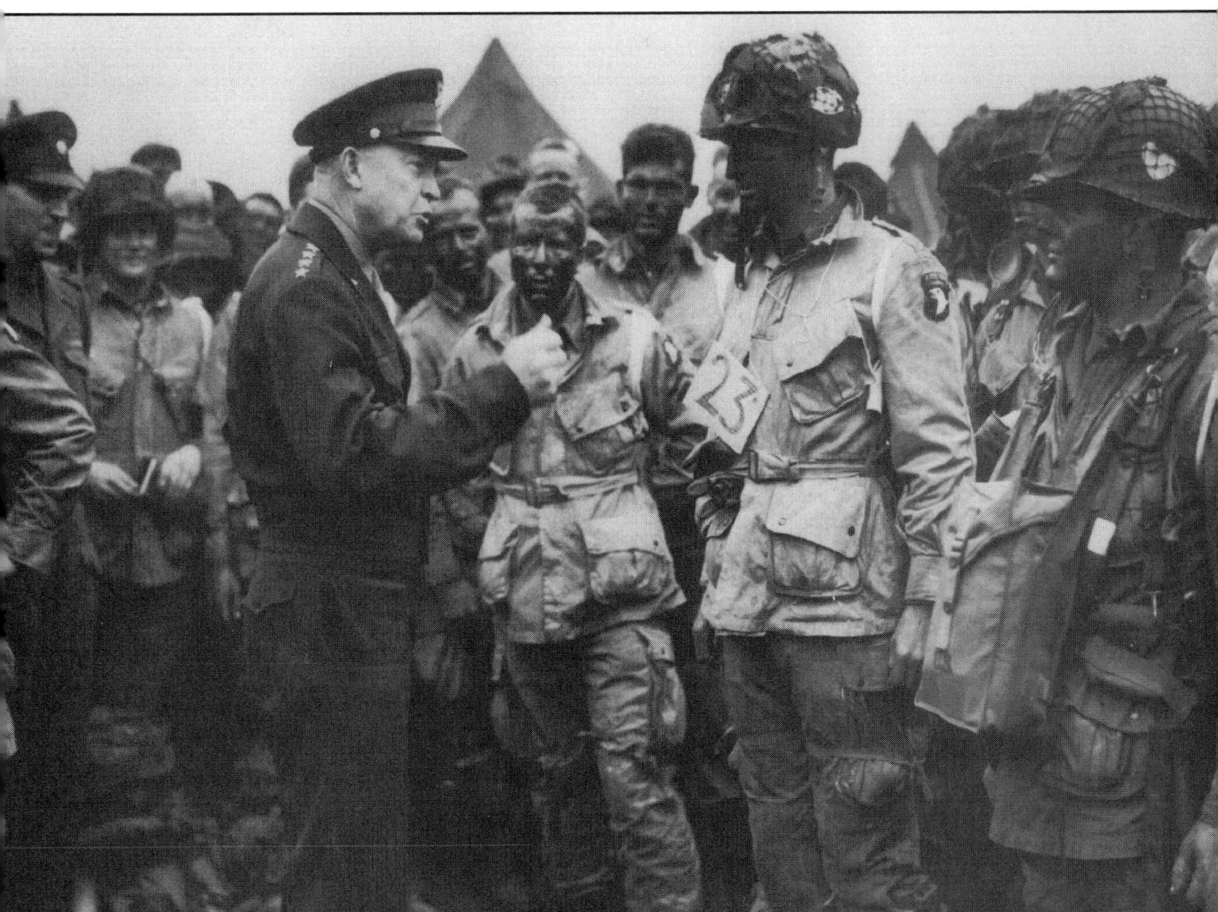

The great advantage of penicillin was that doctors could use it to treat a huge variety of bacterial diseases. Before the discovery of penicillin, surgeons often had to amputate an infected arm or leg to keep the infection from spreading throughout the entire body. Penicillin, however, could stop many infectious bacteria from reproducing. In addition, it also stopped many other contagious diseases caused by bacteria, such as diphtheria and the sexually transmitted syphilis.

When the world realized the value of penicillin, Alexander Fleming became an instant star. The story of the man who discovered penicillin because a mold spore had landed in one of his experiments fascinated the British press. Soon his story spread all over the world, and everyone wanted to meet and talk with the man who had discovered penicillin. Universities everywhere asked him to speak, and world leaders invited him to visit their countries.

Lost in the shuffle were Howard Florey and Ernst Chain. This neglect by the public was partly due to Florey's attitude. Whereas Fleming enjoyed speaking to the press and traveling, Florey had his secretary tell reporters to go away so he could get on with his work. Most reporters resented that treatment, so they instead interviewed Fleming, who took the time to speak to them. Although Fleming always told reporters that penicillin would not have been developed without Florey and Chain, Fleming was given the total credit for developing penicillin and saving countless lives.

Honors, however, poured in for all three scientists. The British crown knighted Fleming and Florey in 1944 and Chain in 1969. In 1945, the Nobel committee awarded the Nobel Prize in medicine to all three researchers.

Fleming's research continued, and he succeeded Sir Almroth Wright as head of the lab in 1946. Fleming spent his final years touring the world, giving speeches, and receiving honors. His wife, Sareen, died in 1949 and, four years later, he married his colleague Dr. Amalia Voureka. When Alexander Fleming's heart failed on March 11, 1955, leaders from many nations sent notes of sympathy to Amalia. People from all over the world attended his funeral, and many countries flew their flags at half-mast.

Howard Florey remained at Oxford, heading the department that had made so many tremendous advances in the study of human immunity. Eventually, he became president of the prestigious Royal Society of Great Britain. He died of a heart attack on February 21, 1968.

Ernst Chain left Oxford in 1948 to work in Italy. In 1961, he returned to England to head a new biochemistry department at the University of London. He died on August 12, 1979.

Although some people are allergic to penicillin, the drug remains successful in treating infections. It is still the best available cure for many diseases and the only cure for some. Penicillin also opened the door to the creation of other antibiotics, a type of drug that kills or stops the growth of bacteria in the

Sir Howard Florey (right) shakes hands with Sir Cyril Hinshelwood, whom Florey succeeded as president of the Royal Society of Great Britain in 1960.

body. Different antibiotics act on different kinds of bacteria. Antibiotics brought a new era to medicine. Without Fleming's observant eye and the determination of Howard Florey and Ernst Chain, this may never have happened.

One serious problem faced by scientists today is that many antibiotics are becoming less effective. After the discovery of penicillin, the public saw antibiotics as wonder drugs—perfect cures that could stop many diseases quickly and safely. Doctors dreamed that one day there would be antibiotics for all dangerous bacteria. They did not realize that even those diseases most easily treated by antibiotics would begin to mutate and become resistant to the drugs.

An example of a disease that may have mutated and become resistant to antibiotics is tuberculosis. Tuberculosis, or TB, was a killer for centuries before Selman A. Waksman developed a new antibiotic called streptomycin in 1944. Afterward, doctors believed that tuberculosis would never claim another human victim. Streptomycin and other antibiotics were so effective against TB that for decades it became 100 percent treatable. In the 1980s, however, incidents of TB began to rise instead of fall. In the 1990s, one TB outbreak afflicted nearly 400 students in a California school. At least 12 of those students had a form of TB that was highly resistant to all known antibiotics.

Much of the problem has arisen because people have taken antibiotics at the slightest sign of illness. Disease-causing bacteria have become so exposed to these antibiotics that bacteria have had ample opportunity to develop ways to resist them. Also, since antibiotics wipe out harmless bacteria as well as disease-causing bacteria, many of the harmless bacteria in our bodies have developed defense systems that can destroy the antibiotic before it ever reaches a disease-causing bacteria.

One day, scientists may develop new ways of fighting bacteria. Until then, the challenge for the future is to stay one step ahead of bacteria with new antibiotics and to use care in prescribing them.

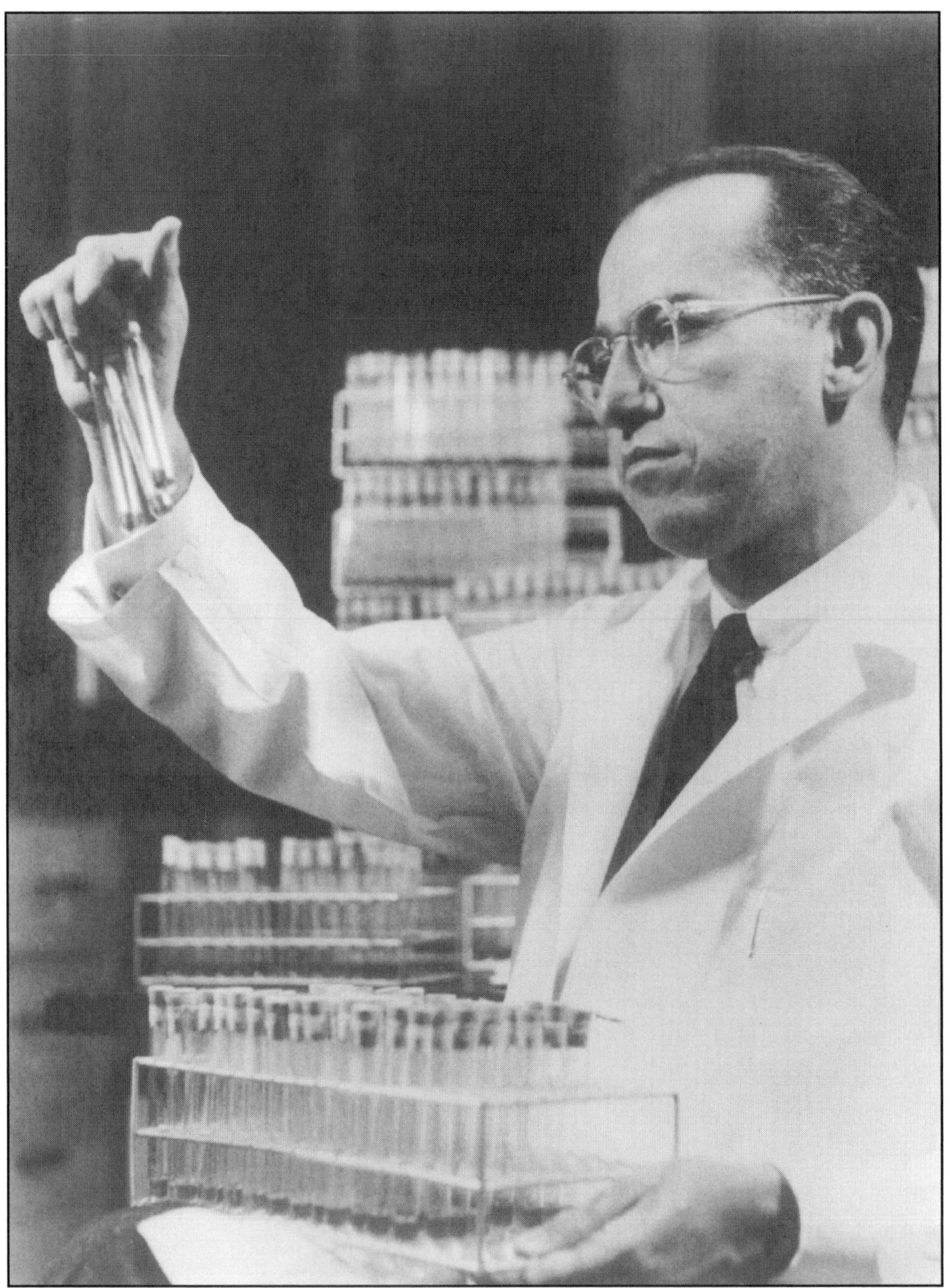

CHAPTER SEVEN

Jonas Salk and the Polio Vaccine

Large cities used to be very dirty places. Drinking water was impure, garbage lay everywhere, and rats and fleas were common. Because of these conditions, cities were the perfect places for viruses and bacteria to grow and flourish. Fortunately, as people began to clean up their cities in the nineteenth and twentieth centuries, many diseases became far less common. Until Jonas Salk developed a vaccine in the 1950s, however, the opposite was true for the disease poliomyelitis, which was also called infantile paralysis, or simply "polio." This disease became more common even as cities began cleaning water supplies and collecting garbage.

During the 1950s, Jonas Salk (1914-1995) became a national hero overnight for developing a vaccine that protected people from the crippling and sometimes fatal disease known as polio.

Jonas Edward Salk was born in New York City on October 28, 1914, to Russian Jewish immigrants Dolly and Daniel Salk. He was the first of their three children. An exceptional student, Jonas excelled in school and entered the City College in New York City at age 15. In his first year there, he enjoyed his chemistry class so much that, following graduation, he went on to study at the New York University School of Medicine.

Most medical students look forward to graduation so they can become doctors. Salk, however, was interested in research, for he was fascinated with viruses. He had been impressed with the work of Thomas Francis Jr., a microbiologist deeply involved with virus research and the search for a vaccine for influenza, or flu.

The day after he graduated from medical school in 1939, Salk married Donna Lindsay. Their three sons—Peter, Darrell, and Jonathan—would also enter the field of medicine.

Salk interned at Mount Sinai Hospital in New York City until 1942. Then he began working at the University of Michigan with Tom Francis, his former teacher. Together, they developed several vaccines against influenza that were used by U.S. soldiers during World War II. In 1947, Salk moved again, this time to the University of Pittsburgh School of Medicine, where he headed his own laboratory. It was here that he began his fight against polio.

Polio was a common infection of the intestinal tract. Ninety to ninety-five percent of the people who contracted polio had flu-like symptoms for a short time. Many didn't realize they had the disease because the symptoms were so mild. If the disease passed through the lymph node system, however, it entered the blood stream and was carried to the central nervous system, causing paralysis of the arms or legs and even death if the lungs were paralyzed.

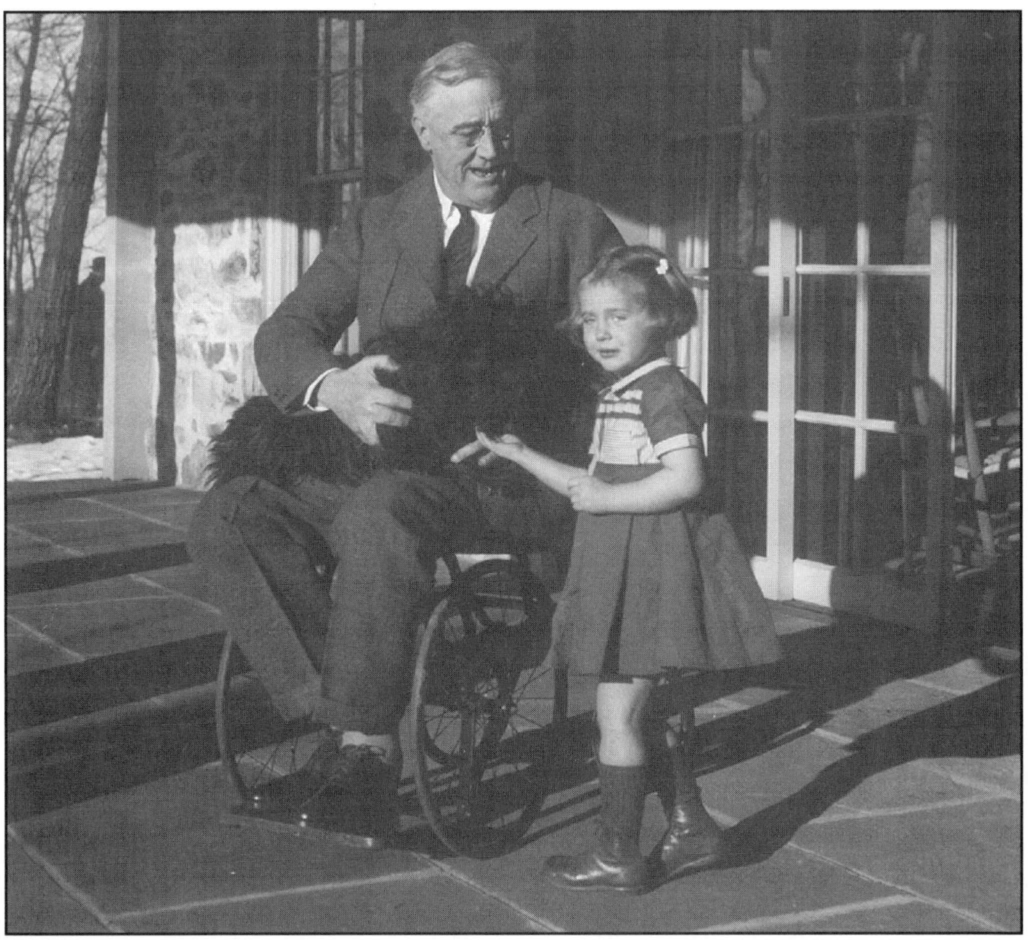

The most famous polio victim was Franklin Delano Roosevelt, who was president of the United States from 1933 to 1945. He contracted polio in 1921 while on vacation at his summer home on Campobello Island in Canada, off the coast of Maine. Although he regained the use of his arms, President Roosevelt could not walk without a cane or crutches and had to wear braces on his legs.

President Franklin Delano Roosevelt (1882-1945) used a wheelchair or leg braces and crutches after his bout with polio in 1921. He is pictured with his dog, Fala, and Ruthie Bie, granddaughter of the caretaker of Roosevelt's home.

Before an epidemic of polio paralyzed 44 people in Stockholm, Sweden, in 1887, severe cases of the disease were uncommon. There is evidence, however, that polio has been around for thousands of years. It was never a serious problem because people normally caught polio when they were infants and their immune systems could handle the disease easily. A person can only contract polio once; after that, the body learns how to fight the disease. As a result, those who were exposed as infants became immune for life. As cities became cleaner, however, people were less apt to be exposed to the disease in infancy, but rather later in life when it was more dangerous.

After the outbreak in Sweden, polio epidemics became more and more common. By the 1950s, more than 50,000 people in the United States alone were catching polio each year. Interest in finding a vaccine to fight polio had been growing throughout the twentieth century. In 1938, President Roosevelt had established the National Foundation for Infantile Paralysis, or NFIP, to fund research. The NFIP then established the March of Dimes and asked Americans to send their dimes to the White House to help raise money to combat polio. In 1938, the March of Dimes collected close to $2 million for polio research. By 1955, they were raising nearly $67 million a year.

Although no cure existed for polio, Sister Elizabeth Kenny, an Australian nurse, had practiced physical therapy for the disease. Kenny began treating polio patients in 1910. At that time, most people

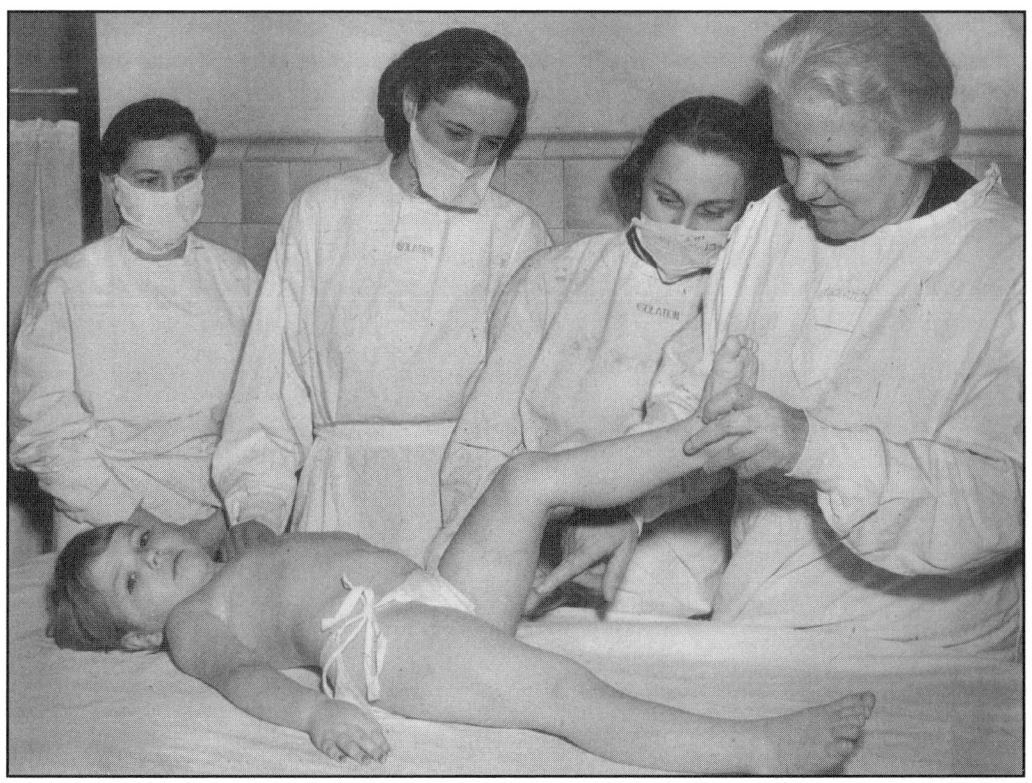

The Elizabeth Kenny Institute was dedicated in Minneapolis, Minnesota, in December 1942. Here Sister Elizabeth Kenny (1880-1952) treated many polio patients and taught her methods of physical therapy to others. The institute merged with Abbott-Northwestern Hospital in 1975, but the hospital's rehabilitation unit still bears Kenny's name.

thought the best way to treat paralysis was to keep polio victims from moving their paralyzed limbs. Kenny disagreed. She told her patients to exercise their arms or legs as much as possible so that the muscles would retain some strength, and she used warm, wet towels to help relax the muscles. Her techniques kept many patients from becoming completely paralyzed.

Before a vaccine could be found, however, researchers needed to know if polio was caused by more than one type of virus. Although they were not sure, they believed that three types of the virus existed. But they did know that any vaccine they developed would have to protect a patient from all types of the virus.

Iron lungs like these at Haynes Memorial Hospital in Boston kept polio victims alive when they became so paralyzed they could not breathe.

In 1948, the NFIP asked Jonas Salk to organize a team to discover and identify the types of polio virus. Salk accepted the job and determined to use the information he found to develop a vaccine against the crippling disease of polio.

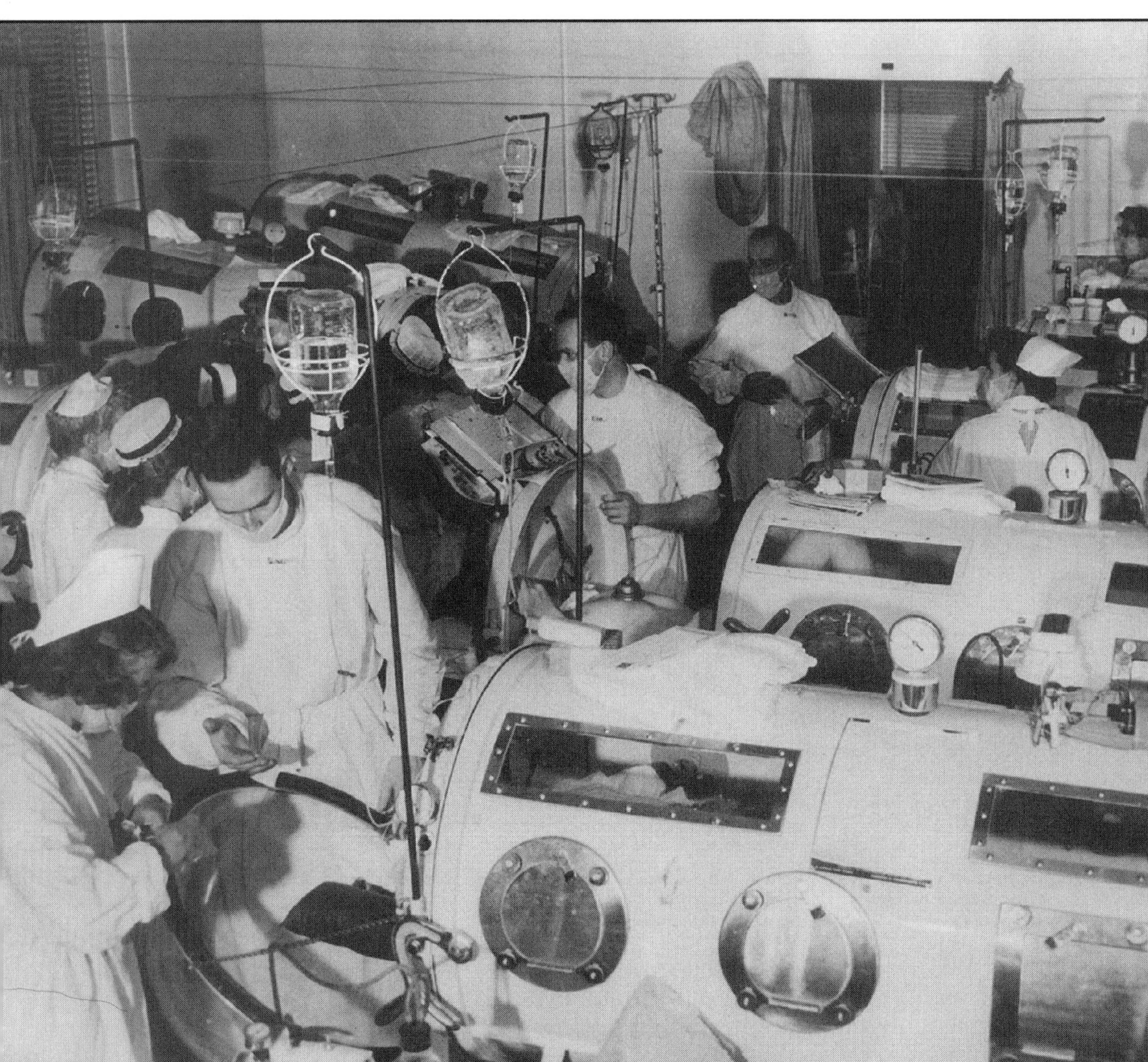

Salk knew that many vaccines use a weakened form of a virus. Injecting the weakened virus into the body taught the body how to resist the disease. Louis Pasteur had first introduced this technique when he weakened a rabies virus to protect people bitten by rabid animals.

Salk believed that he could find a better way to combat polio. Instead of using a weakened virus, he wanted to use a killed virus. Weakened viruses were dangerous because they could regain strength and harm the patient. If a virus were killed, however, it could not possibly cause the disease. But it could still teach the human body to recognize and destroy that virus.

At that time, most scientists believed that a killed virus offered only partial and temporary protection. It might also not be completely safe. If all of the viruses in the vaccine were not killed, the patient might catch polio from the vaccine.

Undaunted, Salk set out to prove that a killed virus vaccine was the safest approach to prevent polio. Even if he failed, he knew that other scientists could learn from his experiments. Salk realized that if researchers were going to beat polio, they had to explore every possible solution.

THE BREAKTHROUGH

Two important breakthroughs set the stage for the Salk vaccine. The first was an experiment carried out by Isabel Morgan. In 1948, Morgan made a polio vaccine with a killed polio virus. She injected the vaccine into several monkeys and found that they became completely immune to polio.

Isabel Morgan made polio vaccine with a killed virus that successfully protected monkeys. This was one of several discoveries that led to the Salk vaccine that worked in human beings.

By itself, however, Morgan's discovery could not lead to a vaccine for humans. Monkeys had a greater natural resistance to polio than humans did, so a weak vaccine that would protect monkeys might not protect humans. More importantly, the only known way to grow the virus was in living nerve tissue of people or monkeys. Researchers knew that viruses grown that way had dangerous side effects in human beings.

The second important breakthrough came in 1949. Working with Thomas Weller and Frederick Robbins, John Enders developed a method of growing the polio virus in tissue from stillborn human embryos. Now researchers could grow the virus safely. For their accomplishment, Enders, Weller, and Robbins received the 1954 Nobel Prize in medicine.

Enders's innovation allowed Salk to experiment on a vaccine for use in humans. Salk later said about Enders, "He threw a forward pass and I caught it."

By the summer of 1950, Salk was convinced that three types of polio virus did exist. He then announced to the NFIP that he was going to work on a vaccine based on a killed virus. Even though

Bacteria had been grown in petri dishes since the 1880s, but viruses could not grow outside a living organism until John Franklin Enders (1897-1985) discovered a medium. Using tissue scraps laced with antibiotics to kill bacteria, he successfully grew the polio virus in 1949.

many other scientists thought this effort would be a waste of time, the NFIP granted Salk the money to begin his experiments.

Salk's toughest task was to find a sure way to kill the virus. Each vaccine shot would contain thousands of polio viruses, and he had to be sure to kill all of them. If he went too far and completely destroyed the viruses, however, then they would not teach the body how to fight the disease.

Salk tried exposing the viruses to ultraviolet light, but this did not kill them all. He decided that the best method was to kill them with formalin, which was the same chemical Morgan had used in her experiments.

Occasionally, one of the doctors at Pittsburgh Municipal Hospital would ask for Salk's help in diagnosing a polio patient. These trips affected him greatly because he would see many young paralyzed children, some of them dying. Soon, the vaccine problem began to consume all of Salk's time and mental efforts. Even on the odd occasion when he went to the movies with his wife, he would still think about his experiments. He knew that more American children were dying from polio than from any other contagious disease.

On June 12, 1952, Salk contacted the director of the D. T. Watson Home for Crippled Children to see if some of the children there might volunteer to test his vaccine. Worried that he had not yet perfected the polio vaccine, Salk did not want to put any healthy volunteers in danger of catching the dreaded disease. The volunteers from the D. T. Watson Home already had polio so his vaccine could not harm them. Even though Salk knew there was no further risk to the children, he later recalled, "When you inoculate children with a polio vaccine, you don't sleep well for two or three months."

Salk's young patients felt no ill effects from the vaccine. In fact, further blood tests showed that the vaccine had stimulated their bodies to produce antibodies, which could destroy invading microorganisms. In short, the vaccine had given the children's bodies a chance to learn how to destroy the polio virus.

The tests done at the Watson Home suggested to Salk that his vaccine was effective. Because his vaccine seemed safe, he could now proceed with trials on people who had never had polio. Because the virus was dead, it could not cause polio. But could the vaccine prevent polio? Salk did not want to use the dangerous approach of vaccinating someone and then injecting that person with live polio virus to see if he or she were immune. He needed a better way.

The NFIP decided to organize the biggest clinical trial in medical history and, to get the clearest results, set up a "double-blind" trial. In this type of clinical testing, half of a large group of volunteers would receive the vaccine and the other half a harmless chemical, or placebo, that looked like the vaccine. The trial would be "double-blind" because neither the doctors who gave the injections nor the volunteers who received them would know which were vaccines or which were placebos.

Next, the researchers would compare the two groups. If the vaccine worked, the group that was vaccinated would have fewer cases of polio than the group that had received the placebo. If the vaccine did not work, then just as many people in the vaccinated group would contract polio as in the placebo group.

The vaccine trials began on April 26, 1954, with Salk himself vaccinating the first volunteer. About 1.8 million children in 44 states, ages five to eight—the age group most vulnerable to polio—participated. Over the next several months, doctors injected more than 600,000 children with the Salk vaccine and just as many with the placebo. The

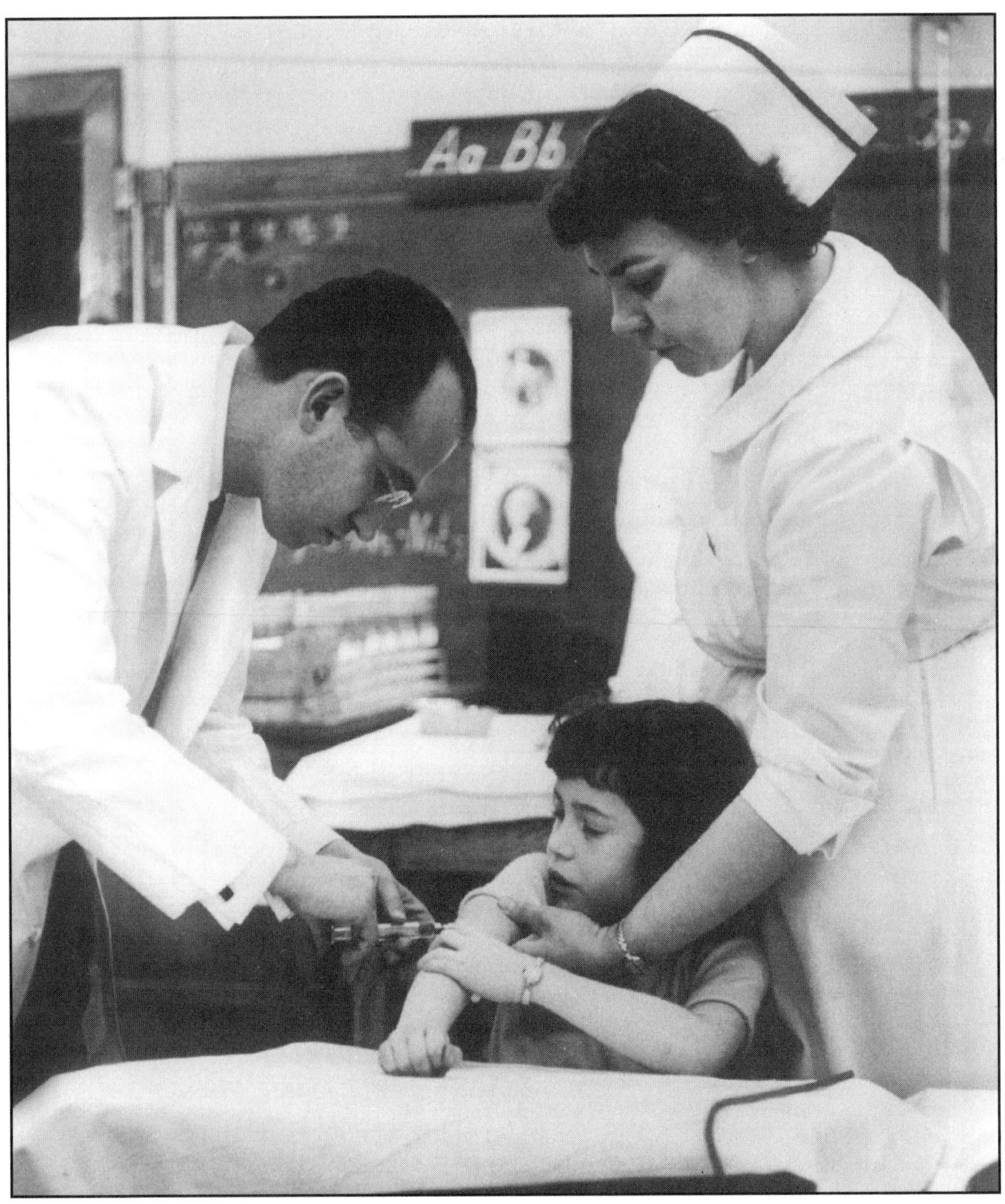

One year before he helped to vaccinate children in the 1954 trials, Jonas Salk had followed an old custom of scientists—he had tried the vaccine on himself, his wife, and their sons.

remaining children were not inoculated at all, but were only observed, and their health was compared to those who had been inoculated. Thomas Francis, Salk's former teacher, agreed to study the results of the trial provided that none of the results would be made public until his team had finished their analysis.

After studying the results of the double-blind trial, Francis called a news conference at the University of Michigan on April 12, 1955, the 10th anniversary of Franklin Roosevelt's death. Hundreds of reporters and scientists crowded the auditorium, waiting for Francis's conclusions. Salk was also present, awaiting the verdict on his work. A hush fell over the crowd as Francis uttered his first words: "The vaccine works!"

Salk was not ready for the fame that awaited him. He awoke on that April morning a scientist, but he went to bed that night a celebrity.

These headlines reporting the announcement that the Salk vaccine worked illustrate how important this news was to people in 1955.

THE RESULTS

Because the results of the trial were so positive, the Food and Drug Administration (FDA), which must approve all drugs sold in the United States, immediately endorsed the production of the Salk vaccine. The FDA licensed six large drug companies to produce the vaccine, and the companies began making it as fast as they could. Because the drug companies could not keep up with the demand for the vaccine, the government decided that doctors could vaccinate only children and pregnant women because they were at the greatest risk. Once an ample supply of vaccine was available, anyone could be vaccinated.

Shortly after the vaccinations began, a disaster occurred that nearly stopped all production of the Salk vaccine. In California, a six-year-old boy contracted polio five days after being vaccinated. Soon, other children came down with polio after receiving the Salk vaccine. Newspapers revealed that two young girls who had been healthy when they received the vaccine had died from polio soon afterward.

Doctors had carefully kept records of every person who had received a vaccination and soon discovered that all of the victims had received a vaccine made by Cutter Laboratories. In producing the vaccine, these labs had not successfully killed all of the polio viruses. The government quickly recalled all of the Salk vaccine manufactured at Cutter Labs, and vaccinations continued throughout the country with vaccine from other labs. Sadly, however, 204 people

These "polio pioneers" were among the almost two million children who participated in the testing of the Salk vaccine.

contracted polio from the Cutter vaccine before it was recalled by the government.

Aside from the Cutter incident, the vaccination program in the United States was a complete success. In 1952, before the Salk vaccine, health officials recorded 57,879 new cases of polio. In 1961, six years after the introduction of the vaccine, there were only 1,300 cases in the entire country.

Scientists were still concerned, however, about how long the protection would last. Nobody could say for sure whether immunity from a vaccine made from a killed virus would last a lifetime.

In 1961, Albert Sabin introduced a vaccine made with a weakened, not killed virus. This new vaccine had two advantages over the Salk vaccine. Unlike the Salk vaccine, the Sabin vaccine required no shots. Instead, people ate sugar cubes coated with the vaccine. Also, it provoked a more powerful immune response which not only protected those who were vaccinated, but also kept them from spreading the disease should they become exposed. Those vaccinated with the Salk vaccine were protected, but they could still be a carrier and infect those not inoculated.

Albert Sabin (1906-1993) developed a vaccine from a weakened polio virus that was the preferred choice of doctors for many years. Each year, however, about six babies contract polio from the Sabin vaccine. In October 1995, The Centers for Disease Control in Atlanta recommended that infants first be inoculated two times with the killed-virus vaccine, then twice more with the live-virus vaccine. Experts hope this will eliminate most cases of vaccine-related polio.

Although polio has been declared eradicated in the Western Hemisphere, about 10,000 children in India are still afflicted each year. On December 9, 1995, the Indian government vaccinated 75 million children under age three in an attempt to control the disease. Bangladesh, Sri Lanka, and Pakistan have begun similar vaccination campaigns. This is the only area of the world still battling polio, but World Health Organization experts said the disease could spread to other parts of the world if the current efforts in India and south Asia fail to reach enough children.

Jonas Salk found fame to be a mixed blessing. Although seeing his image on television and his name in the newspapers was exciting, he now had little privacy. Moreover, some scientists criticized him for getting too much of the credit for the vaccine, saying he had only built on the earlier work of scientists such as Morgan and Enders. But Salk had been the only researcher who had taken advantage of these discoveries, creating a vaccine that worked. The public loved him and named schools and streets in his honor. In the 1950s, one opinion poll ranked him with Winston Churchill and Mahatma Gandhi as a hero of modern history.

In 1955, Jonas Salk received the Congressional Gold Medal and, in 1977, he was awarded the Presidential Medal of Freedom. The Salk Institute for Biological Studies opened in 1963 in San Diego, California, with Salk himself as its director. By the 1990s, the Salk Institute employed more than 500 scientists and staff members.

Salk went on to champion programs that provided vaccinations to children all over the world. In 1986, he and a group of fellow scientists formed a group to study the problems of preventing disease in developing nations.

In 1970, two years after divorcing his first wife, Salk married Françoise Gilot, the onetime companion and inspiration to artist Pablo Picasso. In the mid-1980s, Salk became immersed in the search for the cure to another dreaded disease—Acquired Immune Deficiency Syndrome, or AIDS—and tried the same approach he had successfully used against

Jonas Salk returned to his laboratory at the University of Michigan on April 12, 1995, to celebrate the 40th anniversary of the announcement that his vaccine was successful.

polio: a killed virus vaccine. But his efforts were unsuccessful.

When Jonas Salk died of heart failure on June 23, 1995, *Time* magazine began his obituary by saying: "One good way to assess the great figures of medicine is by how completely they make us forget what we owe them. By that measure, Dr. Jonas E. Salk ranks very high."

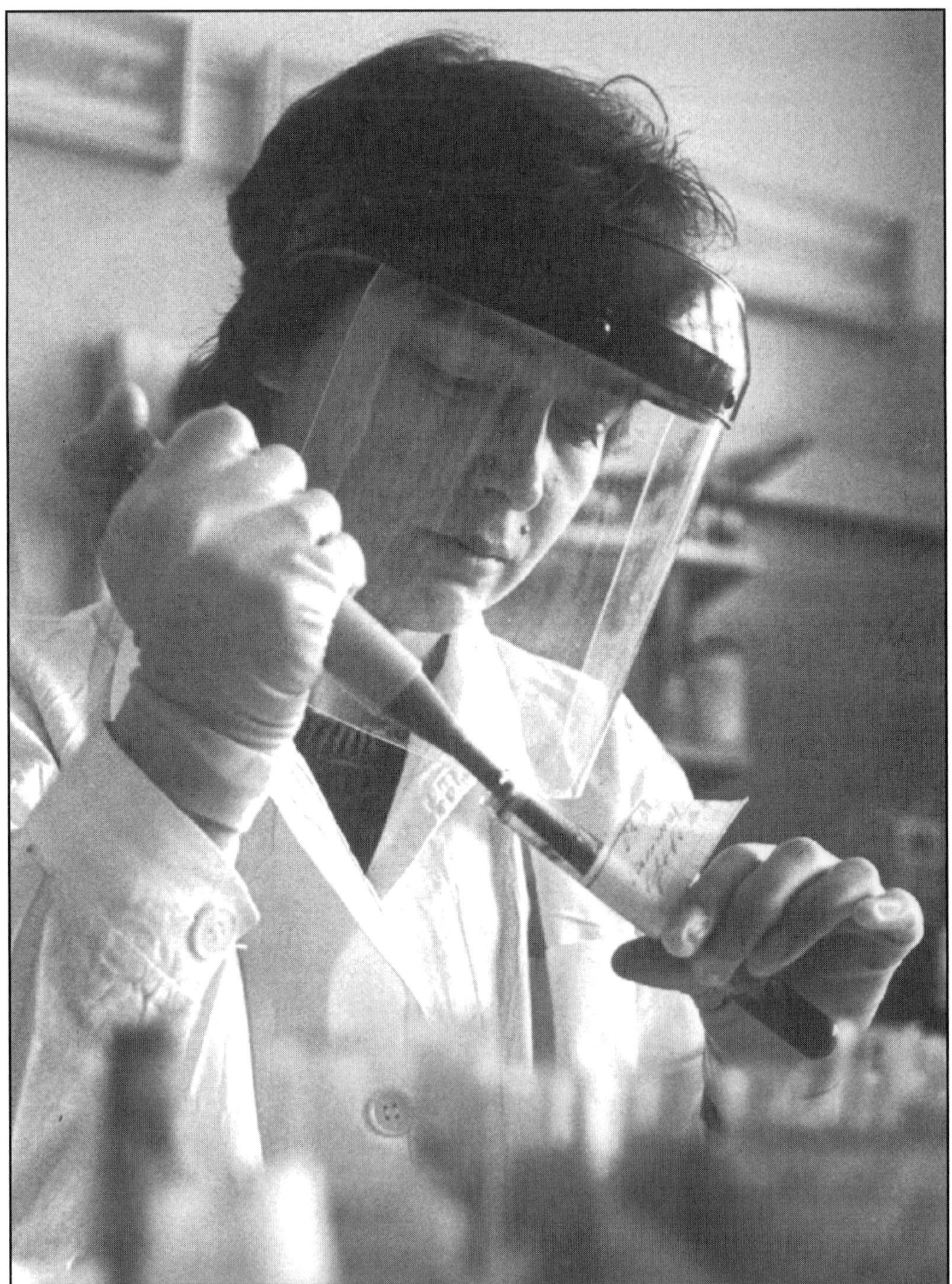

AFTERWORD

AIDS—The Newest Plague

In 1981, Dr. Joel Weisman found that five of his patients in San Francisco were dying because their immune systems had broken down. Without a healthy immune system, the human body has no way to fight off diseases. All five of these patients were young, homosexual males between the ages of 29 and 36. The coincidence was too great to ignore. When reports of similar cases came from New York City, scientists speculated that a new disease had struck the United States. By the end of 1981, 10 people had died from this strange disease. By the end of 1991, 10 years later, 150,114 Americans had died of the disease, and over 1 million more had been infected. In 1982, the scientists had given this disease a name: AIDS, which stands for Acquired Immune Deficiency Syndrome.

A virus called Human Immunodeficiency Virus, or HIV, causes AIDS. HIV is fragile. It dies when exposed to air and can be spread only through

An AIDS researcher in Moscow wears a protective mask and gloves. The city of Moscow hosted the World Health Organization conference on AIDS in March 1989. There have been several such international forums on AIDS, giving researchers across the world the opportunity to share new information and to work together to find a cure.

the exchange of certain body fluids. This means that a person cannot contract HIV through the air or by simply touching someone who has AIDS. An individual can, however, become infected by having unprotected sex with someone infected with HIV or by sharing drug needles with someone who is infected with the virus. Pregnant women can pass the disease on to their children while they are still in the womb. Since HIV lives in the bloodstream, people can also get it from a blood transfusion. This is extremely rare, however, because blood banks now screen all donated blood for HIV.

HIV invades the cells of the human immune system. Once it establishes itself in the immune system, it may take several years before there are any noticeable effects. In fact, a person can be infected for up to 12 years without knowing that he or she carries the virus. Eventually, however, the immune system begins to falter. As it fails, the body becomes especially vulnerable to diseases such as pneumonia, tuberculosis, and endocarditis, an infection of the heart's lining. People are said to have full-blown AIDS instead of HIV when their immune systems fail and they start to contract diseases.

No one knows how HIV began. Scientists speculate that the disease developed in animals. It then spread to humans when an infected animal was killed for food and the animal's blood entered the human bloodstream.

Evidence shows that HIV may have existed in Africa as early as the 1950s. In 1966, a Norwegian sailor who had visited many African seaports in the late 1950s and early 1960s began to show signs that his immune system was breaking down. A year later, his wife showed similar symptoms and, by 1969, their two-year-old daughter was also ill. All three died in 1976. Not knowing what to make of the disease, doctors froze samples of their blood for future research. In the 1980s, when AIDS was better understood, Norwegian doctors tested the blood of each of the three dead people and found that all the samples tested positive for HIV.

Actor Rock Hudson died from AIDS in 1985. He is pictured here three months before his death with actress Doris Day, his costar in many movies.

Many Americans dismissed the significance of AIDS because it seemed to affect only small segments of the U.S. population, such as drug users or homosexual men. But when the popular actor Rock Hudson, who was homosexual, died of the disease on October 2, 1985, people began to pay more attention to the epidemic. In 1991, when Los Angeles Laker basketball star Earvin "Magic" Johnson announced he had HIV, which he attributed to his promiscuity, people became even more aware of the risk of contracting AIDS through casual sexual relations.

"It can happen to anybody, even me, Magic Johnson," said the NBA star at a November 7, 1991, press conference, where he announced he had HIV.

Experts estimate that if no cure for AIDS has been found by the year 2000, 40 million people around the world will have HIV. A cure has been very difficult to find because the virus mutates quickly. As soon as scientists discover a drug that seems to have a positive effect on the disease, HIV mutates into a strain that is resistant to the drug.

This fast mutation rate also makes vaccination ineffective. The virus changes so quickly that the AIDS virus a person is vaccinated against may be radically different from the AIDS virus he or she

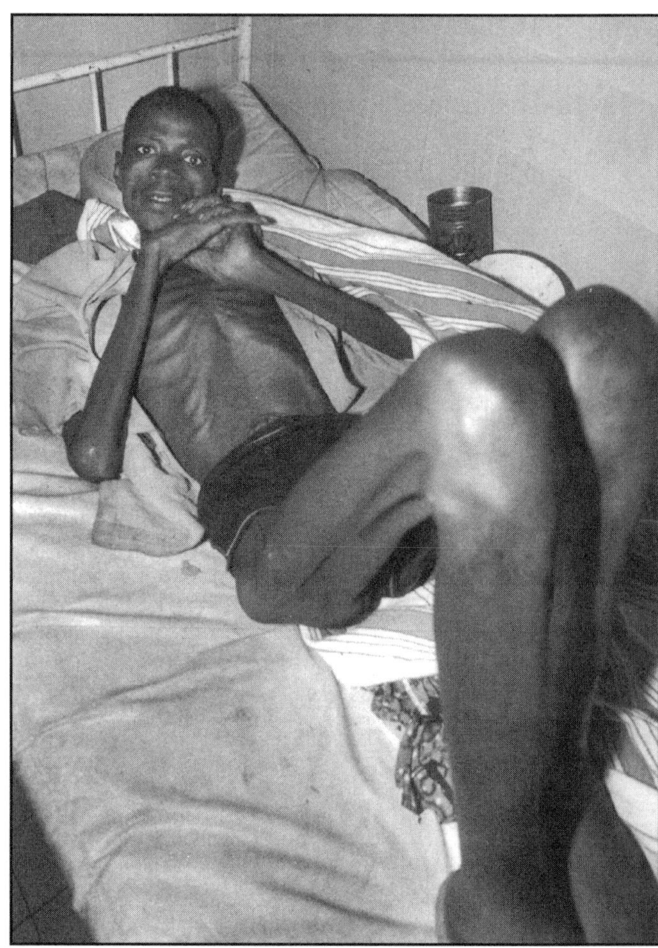

This 36-year-old AIDS victim died a few days after being photographed in a hospital in Abidjan, Ivory Coast. Of the estimated 17 million people reported to have HIV around the world in 1995, more than 11 million—almost 65 percent—live on the continent of Africa.

encounters. Another problem is that scientists have not yet solved many of the mysteries about how HIV attacks the human body.

Scientists now suspect that the answer to HIV lies in basic science. After a decade of little success in trying to find an AIDS cure, scientists in the mid-1990s began to spend less time trying to find a miracle drug to cure the disease and more time studying the virus itself. They realized that the only way to find a cure for the disease would be to understand it thoroughly.

In a way, this is a new approach to finding a cure. Jonas Salk was not worried about studying polio; instead, he cared only about finding a cure as fast as possible. As a result, scientists know little about the polio virus because once Salk found a cure for the disease, there was no need to continue their study of polio. The truth is that every researcher wants to hit a home run and find a cure for any given disease as soon as possible, but this approach may not work against such complex diseases as AIDS and cancer.

In the late 1800s, Louis Pasteur proved beyond a doubt that sickness is caused by tiny microorganisms. The germ theory of disease led to a wave of new cures, ranging from salvarsan to the Salk vaccine. This theory led to a revolution in medicine. Now, with new challenges facing scientists, perhaps another revolution will provide miracle cures to today's dangerous diseases.

Until then, thanks to medical science, people are now living healthier and longer lives than at any time before in history. Science is a powerful tool that helps us trust our own powers of observation, and it provides new solutions to old problems. Most of all, however, science teaches us how much more there is to learn about the universe. Because so many answers still elude us, we know that many of our greatest scientific breakthroughs await us in the future.

At age 14, Ryan White returned to school in Kokomo, Indiana, on April 10, 1986, after a judge removed a restraining order that had kept Ryan from attending school. The school district and some parents had been frightened that Ryan could infect other children with AIDS. Ryan's case helped to educate people about how AIDS is spread and to ensure that AIDS patients don't suffer the additional indignity of losing their civil rights. Born a hemophiliac, Ryan needed many blood transfusions and contracted the disease from contaminated blood. He died on April 8, 1990, at the age of 18.

NOBEL PRIZE WINNERS IN PHYSIOLOGY AND MEDICINE

Names in **bold** are people who are profiled in this book.
Names in ***bold italics*** are people who are mentioned in this book.

1901 Emil A. von Behring—serum therapy against diphtheria
1902 Ronald Ross—work on malaria
1903 Niels R. Finsen—treatment of lupus vulgaris, a rare form of TB
1904 Ivan P. Pavlov—physiology of digestion
1905 ***Robert Koch***—work on tuberculosis
1906 Camillo Golgi and Santiago Ramón y Cajal—structure of the nervous system
1907 ***Charles L.A. Laveran***—protozoa in disease
1908 **Paul Ehrlich** and ***Elie Metchnikoff***—work on immunity
1909 Emil Theodor Kocher—work on thyroid gland
1910 Albrecht Kossel—chemistry of the cell
1911 Allvar Gullstrand—dioptrics (refraction of light) of the eye
1912 Alexis Carrel—grafting blood vessels and organs
1913 Charles Richet—work on hypersensitive reactions to food or drug
1914 Robert Bárány—physiology of vestibular system
1915-1918 NO AWARDS
1919 Jules Bordet—immunity
1920 August Krogh—regulation of capillaries motor mechanism
1921 NO AWARD
1922 Archibald V. Hill—heat production in muscles
Otto Meyerhof—oxygen use and lactic acid production in muscles
1923 **Frederick G. Banting** and **John J. R. Macleod**—discovery of insulin
1924 Willem Einthoven—discovery of electrocardiogram
1925 NO AWARD
1926 Johannes Fibiger—discovery of Spiroptera carcinoma
1927 Julius Wagner-Jauregg—treatment of dementia paralytica
1928 Charles Nicolle—work on typhus exanthematicus
1929 Christiaan Eijkman—discovery of antineuritic vitamins
Frederick G. Hopkins—discovery of growth-promoting vitamins
1930 Karl Landsteiner—discovery of human blood groups
1931 Otto H. Warburg—respiratory work

1932 ***Charles Sherrington*** and Edgar D. Adrian—function of the neuron
1933 Thomas H. Morgan—discovery of hereditary function of chromosomes
1934 George H. Whipple and George R. Minot and William P. Murphy
liver therapy against anemias
1935 Hans Spemann—embryonic development
1936 Henry H. Dale and Otto Loewi—transmission of nerve impulses
1937 Albert Szent-Györgyi von Nagyrapolt—biological combustion
1938 Corneille Heymans—respiration
1939 ***Gerhard Domagk***—antibacterial effect of prontocilate
1940-1942 NO AWARDS
1943 Henrik Dam and Edward A. Doisy—analysis of Vitamin K
1944 Joseph Erlanger and Herbert Spencer Gasser—functions of nerve threads
1945 **Alexander Fleming** and **Ernst Boris Chain** and **Howard W. Florey**
discovery of penicillin
1946 Herman J. Muller—effects of X-rays on genes
1947 Carl F. Cori and Gerty T. Cori—animal starch metabolism
Bernardo A. Houssay—study of pituitary
1948 Paul H. Mueller—insect-killing properties of DDT
1949 Walter Rudolph Hess—brain control of body
Antonio Caetano de Abreu Freire Egas Moniz—brain operation
1950 Philip S. Hench and Edward C. Kendall and Tadeus Reichstein
hormones of adrenal cortex
1951 Max Theiler—vaccine against yellow fever
1952 ***Selman A. Waksman***—co-discovery of streptomycin
1953 Fritz A. Lipmann and Hans Adolph Krebs—studies of living cells
1954 ***John F. Enders*** and ***Thomas H. Weller*** and ***Frederick C. Robbins***
cultivation of polio virus
1955 Hugo Theorell—oxidation enzymes
1956 Dickinson W. Richards, Jr. and André F. Cournand and Werner Forssmann
new ways to treat heart disease
1957 Daniel Bovet—developed allergy and muscle relaxing drugs
1958 Joshua Lederberg—genetic mechanisms
George W. Beadle and Edward L. Tatum
how genes transmit hereditary characteristics

1959 Severo Ochoa and Arthur Kornberg—compounds within chromosomes

1960 Macfarlane Burnet and Peter Brian Medawar
discovery of acquired immunological tolerance

1961 Georg von Bekesy—mechanisms of stimulation within cochlea

1962 James D. Watson and Maurice H. F. Wilkins and Francis H. C. Crick
determined DNA structure

1963 Alan Lloyd Hodgkin and Andrew Fielding Huxley and John Carew Eccles
research on nerve cells

1964 Konrad E. Bloch and Feodor Lynen—cholesterol and fatty acid

1965 François Jacob and André Lwolff and Jacques Monod
regulatory activities in body cells

1966 Charles Brenton Huggins—treatment of prostate cancer
Francis Peyton Rous—discovered tumor-producing viruses

1967 Haldan K. Hartline and George Wald and Ragnar Granit
work on the human eye

1968 Robert W. Holley and Har Gobind Khorana and Marshall W. Nirenberg
studies of genetic code

1969 Max Delbrück and Alfred D. Hershey and Salvador E. Luria
virus infection in living cells

1970 Julius Axelrod and Ulf S. von Euler and Bernard Katz
transmission of nerve impulses

1971 Earl W. Sutherland, Jr.—how hormones work

1972 Gerald M. Edelman and Rodney R. Porter—antibodies

1973 Karl von Frisch and Konrad Lorenz and Nikolaas Tinbergen
behavior patterns

1974 George E. Palade and Christian de Duve and Albert Claude
inner workings of living cells

1975 David Baltimore and Howard M. Temin and Renato Dulbecco
interaction between tumor viruses and genetic material of the cell

1976 Baruch S. Blumberg and D. Carleton Gajdusek—infectious diseases

1977 Rosalyn S. Yalow and Roger C. L. Guillemin and Andrew V. Schally
role of hormones in the body

1978 Daniel Nathans and Hamilton O. Smith and Werner Arber
discovery of restriction enzymes

1979 Allan McLeod Cormack and Godfrey Newbold Hounsfield
developed computed axial tomography (CAT scan) X-ray

1980 Baruj Benacerraf and George D. Snell and Jean Dausset
how cell structures relate to organ transplants and diseases

1981 Roger W. Sperry and David H. Hubel and Torsten N. Wiesel
brain organization and functions

1982 Sune K. Bergström and Bengt I. Samuelsson and John R. Vane
research in prostaglandins, a hormonelike substance involved in illnesses

1983 Barbara McClintock—discovery of mobile genes

1984 Cesar Milstein and Georges J. F. Kohler and Niels K. Jerne
immunology

1985 Michael S. Brown and Joseph L. Goldstein—cholesterol metabolism

1986 Rita Levi-Montalcini and Stanley Cohen
substances that influence cell growth

1987 Susumu Tonegawa—immunological defenses

1988 Gertrude B. Elion and George H. Hitchings and James Black
drug treatment

1989 J. Michael Bishop and Harold E. Varmus—theory of cancer development

1990 Joseph E. Murray and E. Donnall Thomas
pioneering work in transplants

1991 Erwin Neher and Bert Sakmann
developed a technique called patch clamp

1992 Edmond H. Fischer and Edwin G. Kerb—work on enzymes

1993 Richard J. Roberts and Phillip A. Sharp—discovery of split genes

1994 Alfred Gilman and Martin Rodbell
discovered G proteins, a cellular switch crucial to hundreds of processes in the human body

1995 Edward Lewis and Eric Wieschaus and Christiane Nüsslein-Volhard
how genes control embryonic development

GLOSSARY

AIDS: Acquired Immune Deficiency Syndrome, a chronic, incurable, and eventually fatal disease in which HIV (Human Immunodeficiency Virus) causes the immune system to break down, preventing it from fighting off infections. The disease is spread through the exchange of bodily fluids, as in sexual intercourse or drug injections with contaminated needles.

acute: characterized by rapid and severe onset of symptoms

anatomy: the structure of a plant or animal, or the study and science of the structure of a plant or animal

antibiotic: a drug that destroys or limits the growth of microorganisms such as disease-causing bacteria

antibody: a substance produced by the body to destroy, weaken, or neutralize an antigen

antigen: a substance or organism that causes the body to produce an antibody

antisepsis: the destruction or weakening of disease-producing microorganisms to prevent infection

antitoxin: a drug or other substance that prevents or limits the effect of a certain toxin, or poison

atrophy: decrease in size or strength, often said of muscles, due to disease or lack of use

attenuated virus: a virus that has been weakened and made less dangerous

bacteria: microorganisms that can cause disease

bacteriology: the study and science of bacteria, now usually part of microbiology

carbohydrate: any of a group of organic compounds including starches and sugars that provides the main source of energy for the body

cauterize: destroy tissue for medical reasons by burning it with heat, electric current, chemicals

cell: smallest structural unit of an organism that is capable of independent function. It is made up of an outer membrane, the main mass (cytoplasm), and a nucleus.

chemotherapy: the treatment of a disease with chemicals

chronic: characterized by symptoms that develop or recur over a long duration

clinical trial: the testing of a treatment on people

contagious: capable of spreading disease; communicable; infectious

cowpox: a contagious skin disease in cattle, which, when transmitted to humans, makes them immune to smallpox

culture: a deliberate growth of microorganisms in a laboratory

cure: restore to health; or, a treatment that restores health

diabetes: a chronic disorder of the metabolism (the processing of food in the body), due to insufficient production of insulin by the pancreas and characterized by high levels of sugar in the blood and urine. Severe or untreated cases can result in serious health problems.

disease: a disorder with symptoms that results from infection or other cause

distillation: the purification of a liquid by evaporating it and then condensing it again; or, taking out parts of a mixture by heating it and then condensing and collecting its vapors

double-blind trial: a test in which neither the experimenter nor the participant knows whether the participant received the experimental treatment or the placebo (usually water or a sugar pill), so that their expectations for the treatment will not affect the outcome of the experiment

endocarditis: swelling of the membrane (endocardium) lining the inside of the heart and the heart valves due to bacterial infection

endocrine gland: any of several glands that release hormones directly into the bloodstream

enzyme: a protein produced in cells that speeds up the rate of biological reactions

experiment: a test under controlled conditions to see whether a theory is probable or whether a treatment is effective

fermentation: the breakdown of complex substances, such as sugar or other carbohydrates, by enzymes or microorganisms

formalin: a chemical that fights infections and destroys microorganisms

germ theory: the theory that infectious diseases are caused by microorganisms in the body

gland: one of several organs in the human body that releases materials needed by the body

glucose: a sugar common in plant and animal tissue that is the major energy source of the body

HIV: Human Immunodeficiency Virus, the virus that causes AIDS (Acquired Immune Deficiency Syndrome)

hormone: a substance that is produced by one tissue and released into the bloodstream to generate physiological activity, such as growth

immunity: resistance to infection by a certain bacterium or other source

incubation period: the period between the infection by microorganisms such as bacteria or virus and the time that symptoms begin to appear

infection: the invasion of microorganisms such as bacteria or viruses into the body's tissues

inoculation: the introduction of a serum, vaccine, or antigen into the body to boost immunity to a specific disease

insulin: a hormone that regulates the metabolism of carbohydrates and fats

islets of Langerhans: clusters of endocrine cells in the tissue of the pancreas that release insulin into the bloodstream

killed virus: a virus that has been rendered harmless so that it is safe for use in vaccines

lysozyme: an enzyme in egg whites, human tears, saliva, and other bodily fluids that destroys certain bacteria and thus acts as an antiseptic

metabolize: undergo the chemical and physical processes of the transformation of food into energy and other body functions

microbe: a tiny life form, especially a bacterium that causes disease

microbiology: the branch of biology that studies microorganisms and their effects on living organisms

microorganism: a very small organism, usually visible only under a microscope, such as bacteria or fungi

microscope: an instrument that magnifies objects, some invisible to the human eye. A light microscope uses light and a combination of lenses to magnify and focus an object; the electron microscope uses a beam of electrons to scan and produce an image.

mold: a fungus that often causes organic matter to disintegrate

mutation: a sudden structural change in a gene or chromosome of an organism

Mycoderma aceti: tiny organisms that can cause liquids to sour; used to manufacture vinegar

nervous system: an extensive network of cells that conduct information with impulses to control, regulate, and coordinate all the body's functions. The central nervous system is made up of the brain and spinal cord.

Nobel Prize: a highly prestigious international award for achievement in the fields of physics, chemistry, physiology or medicine, literature, and peace

organism: an individual form of life (animal, plant, microorganism, or cell)

pancreas: a gland behind the stomach that releases insulin into the bloodstream and digestive enzymes into the digestive system

paralysis: the loss or impairment of the ability to move a body part, usually as the result of disease or injury to the nervous system

pasteurization: the process of heating or exposing to radiation beverages or food, especially milk, to a specific temperature for a specific period of time to kill microorganisms that could cause disease or spoilage

penicillin: any of a group of antibiotic drugs obtained from penicillium molds or produced synthetically that treat infections and diseases

petri dish: a shallow dish with a loose cover used to grow microorganisms

placebo: a substance (usually water or a sugar pill) that contains no medication that is used in experiments to provide a comparison with the drug or treatment being tested

pneumonia: a disease that is caused by viruses, bacteria, or other microorganisms and characterized by the swelling of the lungs

poliomyelitis: (polio) a highly infectious viral disease affecting the central nervous system which in severe forms results in permanent paralysis or death

pustule: a small, inflamed, and pus-filled swelling on the skin

quarantine: the practice of isolating individuals who are infected with a contagious disease to prevent the spread of the disease

rabies: an acute, infectious, and often fatal viral disease of warm-blooded animals that attacks the central nervous system and is transmitted by the bite of infected animals

salvarsan: a chemical compound that cured syphilis, discovered by Paul Ehrlich in 1909

scurvy: a disease caused by a deficiency of vitamin C and characterized by spongy and bleeding gums and bleeding under the skin. If untreated, scurvy is fatal.

serum: blood serum (the liquid part of blood) of immunized animals that contains antibodies and is used to immunize humans

smallpox: an acute, highly infectious, and often fatal disease caused by a poxvirus and characterized by high fever, aches, and widespread pox (pus-filled swellings on the skin)

spontaneous generation: the supposed development of living organisms from non-living matter

sterilize: remove bacteria and other microorganisms from an object

streptococcus: a bacterium that causes various diseases in humans, including tonsillitis, pneumonia, urinary tract infections, and strep throat

symptom: a sign that indicates the presence of a disorder or disease

syphilis: a chronic infectious disease, which is transmitted by sexual contact, or passed from mother to fetus. If not treated with an antibiotic, syphilis is eventually fatal.

trypanosome: a parasitic protozoan (a single-celled organism that needs a host to live on) that is transmitted to humans by certain insects and causes diseases such as sleeping sickness

tuberculosis: a chronic infectious disease of humans and animals which is characterized by the formation of tubercles (swellings or lesions) in the lungs and other tissues of the body

ultraviolet light: the invisible short-wavelength light in sunlight that tans and burns the skin

vaccinate: inoculate (often by injection) with a vaccine to produce immunity to an infectious disease

vaccine: a weakened or killed bacterium or virus that stimulates the production of antibodies against that bacterium or virus

viral: caused by a virus

virus: a small particle that can reproduce itself with a living cell. It takes over the nucleic acid of the host, reproduces, then bursts the host cell, releasing new virus particles. Derived from the Latin word for poison, viruses cause many human diseases.

vitamin C: a crystalline water-soluble substance that is essential to the normal growth and activity of the body; a deficiency of vitamin C causes scurvy; also called ascorbic acid

BIBLIOGRAPHY

Aaseng, Nathan. *The Disease Fighters: The Nobel Prize in Medicine.* Minneapolis: Lerner, 1987.

Ackerknecht, Erwin H. *A Short History of Medicine.* Baltimore: The Johns Hopkins University Press, 1982.

Baumler, Ernst. *Paul Ehrlich: Scientist for Life.* New York: Holmes & Meier, 1984.

Bliss, Michael. *Banting: A Biography.* Toronto: McClelland and Stewart, 1984.

Bredeson, Carmen. *Jonas Salk: Discoverer of the Polio Vaccine.* Springfield, N.J.: Enslow, 1993.

Bullough, Vern L. "James Lind." *Dictionary of Scientific Biography.*

Burge, Michael C., and Don Nardo. *Vaccines: Preventing Disease.* San Diego: Lucent Books, 1992.

Caldwell, Mark. "Prokaryotes at the Gate." *Discover* (August, 1994): 45-50.

Carter, Richard. *Breakthrough: The Saga of Jonas Salk.* New York: Trident, 1966.

Curtis, Robert H. *Great Lives: Medicine.* New York: Charles Scribner's Sons, 1993.

Gould, Peter. *The Slow Plague.* Cambridge, Mass.: Blackwell, 1993.

Holmes, S. J. *Louis Pasteur.* New York: Dover, 1961.

Hombs, Mary Ellen. *AIDS Crisis in America.* Santa Barbara: ABC-CLIO, 1992.

Hughes, R. E. "James Lind and the Cure of Scurvy: An Experimental Approach." *Medical History* (1975): 342-351.

Kruif, Paul de. *Microbe Hunters.* New York: Harcourt, Brace and Company, 1953.

Lemonick, Michael D. "The Killers All Around." *Time* (September, 1994): 65-69.

Macfarlane, Gwyn. *Alexander Fleming, the Man and the Myth.* London: Oxford University Press, 1985.

Manger, Lois. *A History of Medicine.* New York: Marcel Dekker, 1992.

Marquardt, Martha. *Paul Ehrlich.* London: William Heinemann Medical Books, 1949.

McGrew, Roderick E. *Encyclopedia of Medical History.* New York: McGraw-Hill, 1985.

Nardon, Don. *The Irish Potato Famine.* San Diego: Lucent Books, 1990.

Nicolle, Jacques. *Louis Pasteur: A Master of Scientific Enquiry.* London: Hutchinson & Co., 1961.

Plotkin, Stanley A., and Susan L. Plotkin. "Vaccination: One Hundred Years Later." In *World's Debt to Pasteur,* edited by Hilary Koprowski and Stanley A. Plotkin. New York: Alan R. Liss, 1985.

Roddis, Louis H. *James Lind: Founder of Nautical Medicine.* New York: Henry Schuman, 1950.

Rytel, Michael W., and William J. Mogabgab. *Clinical Manual of Infectious Diseases.* Chicago: Year Book Medical, 1984.

White, Ryan and Ann Marie Cunningham. *Ryan White: My Own Story.* New York: Dial Books, 1991.

Wilson, Leonard G. "The Clinical Definition of Scurvy and the Discovery of Vitamin C." *Journal of the History of Medicine and Allied Sciences* (1975): 40-60.

INDEX

ABOUT THE AUTHOR

Robert Mulcahy, born in Brooklyn, N.Y., in 1971, graduated summa cum laude from the University of Minnesota with a degree in literary studies. He now works both as an author and as an instructional developer of educational computer software. He is also the author of *Medical Technology: Inventing the Instruments,* published by The Oliver Press. He lives in St. Paul, Minnesota.

PHOTO ACKNOWLEDGEMENTS

Archive Photos: p. 98.
The Bettmann Archive: pp. 14, 65, 72, 91, 93, 117, 120, 123 (both), 124, 125.
Franklin D. Roosevelt Library: p. 103.
Illustrated London News: p. 24.
J. B. Collip Papers, Thomas Fisher Rare Book Library, University of Toronto: p. 80.
Library of Congress: pp. 6, 7, 9, 11 (both), 12, 17, 26, 37, 38, 40, 43, 46, 57, 61, 68, 84, 95.
March of Dimes Birth Defects Foundation: pp. 13, 100, 106, 109, 112, 114, 116, 119.
National Library of Medicine: pp. 30, 39, 58, 66, 81, 108.
National Aeronautics and Space Administration (NASA): p. 82
Revilo: p. 19.
Roger-Viollet, Paris: pp. 48, 52.
St. Mary's Medical School, London: pp. 88, 90.
***Star Tribune*/Minneapolis-St. Paul:** p. 105.
Stock Montage, Inc.: pp. 34, 55.
University of Toronto Archives: pp. 70, 75, 77, 79, 83.
Warner-Lambert Company: p. 21.